PONIES IN THE WILD

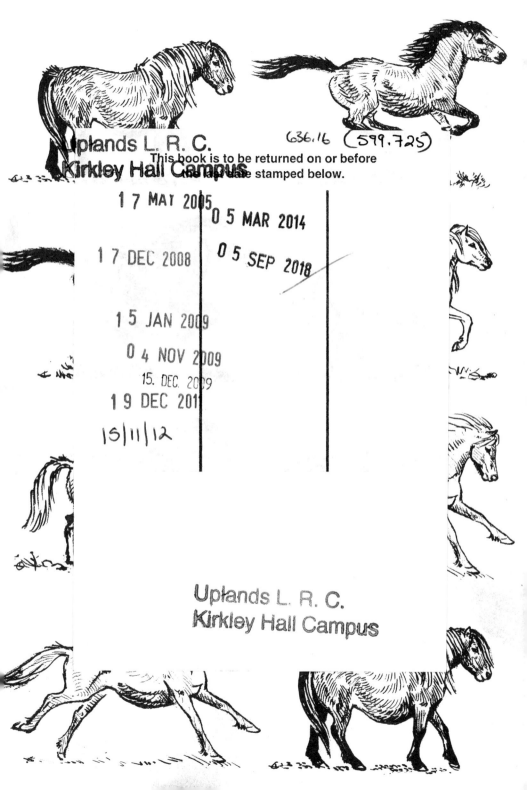

PONIES IN THE WILD

• ELAINE GILL •

with illustrations by
DIANA E. BROWN

Whittet Books

First published 1994
Text © 1994 by Elaine Gill
Illustrations © 1994 by Diana E. Brown
Whittet Books Ltd, 18 Anley Road, London W14 0BY

British Library Cataloguing-in-Publication data. A catalogue record for this book is available from the British Library.
ISBN 1 873580 11 8

Acknowledgments
Many people have been involved in the production of this book and I would like to express warm thanks to the following. David Freemantle and Chris Feare made invaluable comments on the manuscript and were a constant source of encouragement. Information and comments were kindly given by my fellow 'horse-doctors' Sue Baker and Debbie Goodwin, also Julie Bishop, Jim Bowmaker, John Knowles, Graham Martin, Ieuan and Ray Morgan, Sylvia Sikes and the secretaries of the British pony breed societies. I would also like to thank the commoners, especially of the New Forest, for allowing me to become part of their lives for a while, and Shirley Blick and Bill Jones for permission to publish the agister's diary excerpts. Thank you to Diana (artist) who brought a smile to my face with her drawings, to Annabel (publisher) who believed that I could do it, and to my family and friends for their support, and tolerance of my antisocial and obsessive behaviour whilst writing this book. Finally, I would like to thank Rory Putman and Jon Pollock who first launched me into the private lives of ponies – without whom I would not be writing this.

Typeset by Spectrum City
Printed and bound by Biddles of Guildford

Contents

In the beginning	6
Return to the wild?	12
Introducing ... the ponies	14
The British	20
Special equipment	30
A natural group	42
An unnatural group	45
Who's who within the group	48
Moods and messages	52
Between groups	55
Passing the time	57
Horsing around	64
What goes in must come out ...	67
A new generation	71
It's a foal!	77
The milk bar	80
Health and welfare	83
Digestive difficulties	86
Disease	90
Lodgers and visitors	93
Ponies and people	102
The commoners	104
Which is whose?	107
An ecological mowing machine	117
People as pests	120
The future?	123
Further reading	124
Glossary	125
Index	127

In the beginning

Eohippus.

Sixty million years ago in the swamps and river banks of the Eocene World lived an herbivorous mammal the size of a fox with a long tail, four broad toes on each front foot and three on each at the back. Its broad feet allowed it to move easily around its marshy environment where, with small, low-crowned teeth, it browsed the vegetation and probably ate the odd insect or other small animal. This was 'Eohippus'. During the millions of years that followed, the descendants of this soft-footed animal found that they had to cope with firmer, more open ground and that being able to run fast to escape the predators of these areas was a distinct advantage. Some 59 million years later (about 15 million generations), this inconspicuous herbivore has grown taller and, with just a single toe on each foot, is running swiftly over the plains. This is *Equus*.

Today, some 7 or 8 species of *Equus* are recognized within the horse family (or Equidae) and, depending on whose classification you follow, there are between about 14 and 20 subspecies. The family belongs, with tapirs and rhinos, to the mammalian order Perissodactyla, the odd-toed ungulates. The other hoofed mammals, the Artiodactyla or even-toed ungulates, which include cows, sheep, deer, antelope and pigs, may look similar to the members of the Perissodactyla but this is believed to have come about through convergent evolution (see Glossary). The common ancestor of the ungulates lived long before *Eohippus* braved the earth.

Fossil remains suggest that *Equus* originated in North America, some-where around the foothills of the Rocky Mountains in what is now Wyoming. During the Ice Ages of the Pleistocene (about a million years ago), *Equus* migrated across the land bridges that then existed to South America, Europe, Asia and Africa. That was a fortunate move on *Equus'* part, because, as the ice was retreating about 10,000 years ago, the hors-es in North and South America were wiped out. The cause of this sud-den, mass extinction after surviving four geological epochs and nearly 60 million years still remains a mystery. At around the same time rhinoc-eros, camel, sabre-toothed tiger and elephant also disappeared from the Americas, but companion grazers such as the bison thrived. Climate, dis-ease, human interference and inadequate food may all have been partly responsible, but no single factor can be identified as the principal cause.

The family

Today's Equidae family may be divided into four broad groups: wild asses of both Asia and Africa, zebras and horses. The definition of the *Equus* species and subspecies varies depending on whose book you read. The way in which I present them below is just one example, there are many others. All of the species of the Equidae can interbreed, although this rarely happens without man's help; only crosses within the horses produce fertile offspring.

The Asian wild asses, *Equus hemionus*, of which there are at least four subspecies in existence today, are probably the horse's closest rela-tions. This is particularly noticeable in the Tibetan Kiang and the Mongolian Kulan; of all the asses and zebras they look most like horses, with (relatively) small ears and quite broad hooves, and their call is more of a whinny than a bray. Other Asian asses include the Persian Onager and the Indian Ghor-khar. The populations of all these asses are

Relative sizes of Equidae and rhinoceros and a baby tapir.

Kiang, or Tibetan wild ass.

small and their existence is threatened by poaching and competition for space with man and his domestic stock. There was a fifth subspecies, the Syrian wild ass, which became extinct in 1927.

The African wild ass, *Equus asinus*, of which there are three sub-species, Nubian, Somali and African, is the ancestor of the domestic donkey. All three types have the narrow hooves of a donkey, and the Nubian wild ass is particularly small with a donkey-like white muzzle and eye and a stripe down its back and shoulders. They live in the hilly, stony deserts and arid and semi-arid grasslands of Ethiopa, Somalia and the Sudan but, like their Asian relatives, their numbers are declining and the species is threatened by hunting and competition with domestic stock for food and water. Although these asses are now confined to

North Africa, they may have originated in Asia.

There are three species and about six subspecies of zebra living in the plains and mountains of Africa today. The Plains zebra, *Equus burchelli*, is the most abundant zebra in the wild. It lives in the savannahs and woodlands of east, south and central Africa at heights ranging from sea level to 4,000 metres (over 12,000 feet). The species includes Chapman's, Boehm's, Grant's, Damara, Eastern Plains and the now extinct Burchell's zebras. It is a stocky zebra and most subspecies have broad stripes on a creamy-orange background. The Mountain zebra, *Equus zebra*, is uncommon and considered vulnerable to extinction, especially whilst there is a profitable market for its skin, which can fetch up to $500, and meat, which in Namibia is about two-thirds the price of beef. It also competes with domestic stock for food and water. It lives in the mountain grasslands of South-West Africa at heights of up to 2,000 metres (7,000 feet), where frost and snow are common, and is also found in arid regions on the edges of deserts and on semi-arid grassland. Its stripes are narrower than those of the Plains, it has a small dewlap and along its spine the hair points forwards instead of backwards – quite why is not known. The third species, Grevy's zebra – *Equus grevyi* – is the most endangered of the three zebra species – mainly because of the high value of its skin in the past. Although the market for skins ceased in the mid 1970s, when the zebra was listed as endangered, and poaching is now not a problem, few remain today, and of these many compete with domestic stock for resources. If not actively conserved, it is likely to be extinct within fifty years. It is the most northerly zebra, living on the dry, shrubby grassland and subdesert steppe of Ethiopia and northern Kenya. It is the largest of all the zebras (up to 150 cm at the shoulder) with narrow stripes, particularly large ears and, unlike the other zebras, a white belly.

Until the late 1800s there was another sort of zebra. This was *Equus quagga*, the Quagga (some pronounce it 'Kwa-ha' because of the noise it made), a yellowish-brown equid which had the stripes of a zebra on its front end and the plain coat of a horse at the back – although some reportedly also had a few dark spots on the flanks. It was able to live in more arid regions than the other zebras, and was particularly common in South Africa, where it was hunted for food for African workers and later for its hide. It was very docile, unlike the other zebras, and was easily domesticated. In the 19th century it became a fashionable pet, and a pair was frequently seen pulling a phaeton around London! Sadly, its value for meat and skin, combined with its docility, became its downfall

Quagga.

and the last specimen died in captivity in Amsterdam in 1883. A fine (stuffed) example of a Quagga can be seen in the Rothschild Collection at Tring, Hertfordshire, together with one of the few photographs ever to have been taken of the species. At San Diego Zoo (USA) and the South African Museum in Cape Town there have been attempts to recreate the Quagga using DNA extracted from dried blood and skin samples from a preserved Quagga, but no new, man-made Quaggas have appeared so far.

Two species of horse are normally recognized today – *Equus caballus* (also known as *E. ferus*), the 'domestic' horse, and *Equus przewalskii* (pronounced 'shevalski'), the Mongolian 'wild' horse. Although several species of wild horse are known to have existed until the last Ice Age, such as the massive European *E. bressanus* (larger than a Shire horse) and its slightly smaller descendants *E. mosbachensis* and *E. germanicus*, and the 'pigmy' horse, *E. tau*, it is thought that only *E. przewalskii* survived. It is therefore generally believed to be the ancestor of all present-day horses. The most popular theory is that as it spread across Europe and Asia, different types of horse evolved according to the environment in which they lived, so giving rise to the breeds and types we know today.

Przewalski's horse is a strong, sturdy pony with a large head, measuring between 12 and 13 hands (120-130 cm). It is a pale, golden dun colour with an oatmeal coloured nose and ring round the eye, a dark eel stripe down its spine, a distinctive upright, short mane – which, unlike that of *E. caballus*, is shed each spring, so there is not enough time to grow a forelock – and the top of its tail has short, coarse golden hairs, the rest consisting of long, black hairs. Some individuals also have a dark stripe down the shoulder (like a donkey's) and 'zebra stripes' on the legs near the knees and hocks. It was discovered in 1881 in the Tachin Schara Nuru mountains at the edge of the Gobi desert by Colonel Przewalski, a Russian explorer. Unlike *caballus* it does not take kindly to handling or training and is more aggressive both towards humans and its own kind. When, twenty years later, a collector of exotic animals, Karl Hagenbeck, captured thirty-two young horses, he needed the help of no less than 2,000 Kirghiz tribesmen! Most people believe that Przewalski's horse is now extinct in the wild. In 1968 a pair was seen in Mongolia but there have been no confirmed sightings since – although it must be said that it would be easy to miss a few individuals in the vast wastes of Mongolia. Karl Hagenbeck's original specimens bred successfully and became the ancestors of some of the thriving captive populations in zoos and parks today, such as at Woburn Abbey (Bedfordshire), Marwell Zoo (Hampshire), Frankfurt, Leipzig and Munich Zoos (Germany), Prague Zoo (Czechoslovakia) and San Diego Zoo (California), with the largest collection in the Ukraine on a 2,600 hectare (6,400 acre) reserve at Askania Nova, the estate of Baron Friedrich von Falzfein. The total population is currently about 1,200.

Prezewalski's is more aggressive than the domestic horse.

Return to the wild?

For a number of years a group of the zoos and parks that keep and breed Przewalskis have been looking at the feasibility of releasing them back into the wild in Mongolia. This is an exciting project, but one with many biological and sociological hurdles to be overcome. One fundamental problem is that what you select in horses as desirable features for a captive life, such as an amiable temperament (well, relatively), are unlikely to be what would be selected naturally to fit the animal for a life in the wild. Most of the current populations of Przewalski horses have now been captive for many generations; individuals descended from Hagenbeck's specimens, for example, come from stock that has been in captivity for about ninety years – about twenty-five generations. Another problem with introducing the horses into Mongolia is that unless they are securely fenced in, they are likely to interbreed with Mongolian domestic and feral horses – a practice which will not only produce undesirable cross-breeds but also may result in their being shot by the local people. There is a strong will to reintroduce the horses to Mongolia where they hold a cultural value and symbolize the freedom of the country. Private collectors have tried releasing a few horses, but the individuals have sadly either ended up dead or at best no freer than they were in the zoos.

Some progress has been made; in March 1993, a group of 7 Przewalskis – three- to four-old-mares, 1 with a colt foal, and 3 young stallions – from zoos in Britain, Germany and France were released into 300 hectares (740 acres) of remote secondary steppe land, the Causse Méjean, in the Cevennes in southern France. A further 4 or 5 individuals are due to join them in September 1993. This area is hardly the Gobi Desert, but fossil remains suggest that a few thousand years ago it was home to a large population of horses. The individuals were selected to be as genetically different as possible, a challenging task when the total population is descended from only 13 individuals, and they will be left alone to breed as and with whom they will. The aim is to use their offspring for release into the Gobi.

Until recently it was believed that there was another ancestral horse, the Tarpan of North-east Europe. This was a small, mouse-coloured pony also with an eel stripe down its back and an upright mane. It was of a lighter build than the Przewalski and was thought to be the ancestor of the lighter types of horses. However, cave paintings discovered in North-east Europe

Paleolithic cave painting of Przewalski's horse.

depict only Przewalski horses, and it has since been suggested that the Tarpan was of domestic stock, albeit of a primitive type, which had reverted to a wild state. The original Tarpan is now extinct. The last free-living one died in 1879 and the last one in captivity in 1919. Today there are a number of 'New' Tarpans running semi-wild in Polish reserves, bred from captured 'wild' ponies believed to resemble the original.

If there are no wild horses left in the world (apart from a possible few in Mongolia), what are the ponies living 'wild' in Britain in the New Forest, on Dartmoor, Exmoor and the Welsh hills? What are the Mustangs of the western United States and the Brumbies of Australia? These horses and ponies fend for themselves all year, but none is truly wild. The British populations are believed to have originated from ancient British stock and so may be described as 'native' to Britain, but for many hundreds of years most have been owned by someone and have been managed and modified to suit the needs of man. In the rest of the world it is the other way round; most of the larger populations are feral, that is they originate from horses or ponies which escaped from man, but since then have received very little human interference. Natural selection, the survival of the fittest, has been able to act on these feral populations and, having become adapted to their respective environments, they look very different from their captive ancestors.

This is a book about ponies that fend for themselves, so we shall concentrate on the breeds and types that do this today. For simplicity, I have lumped all of the populations under the title which best describes them all – 'free-ranging'. The term 'native' is used to describe populations that are believed to have originated in the country in which they now live. Throughout the book, 'pony', and in the case of larger types, 'horse', will mean 'free-ranging pony' (or horse) unless I specify otherwise.

Introducing . . . the ponies

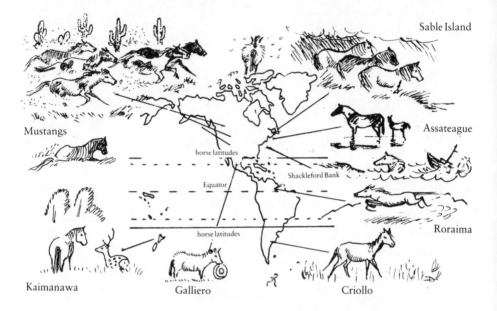

Sable Island

Mustangs

Assateague

horse latitudes

Shackleford Bank

Equator

Roraima

horse latitudes

Kaimanawa

Galliero

Criollo

(Above and opposite) *Free-ranging ponies of the world.* NOTE *horse latitudes are areas of calm in the Atlantic Ocean about 30° north and south. Believed to be so-called because ships became becalmed and had to off-load cargo, especially horses, which drank a lot of water.*

Where do they live?

Our maps show where the best known populations in the world live. Ponies and horses are found in all kinds of terrain, including deserts, mountainous regions, woodland, moorland, saltmarsh and on sandy islands. Some of these populations have been studied in depth, but there are many about which very little is known. The number of populations and the size of many has decreased over the centuries mainly due to pressures from man for space and the need and desire for domesticated horses. Ironically, when man provides food or shelter in times of hardship, this allows the less fit individuals to survive and breed, and ultimately reduces the hardiness of the population.

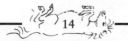

Who are they?
Some of the largest populations in the world live in North America and on islands off its East Coast. It is a strange coincidence that the place from which the original horses were wiped out should now accommodate so many; probably the most famous of which are

MUSTANGS
'Mustang' is the general name for 'wild' horse in the western United States; it is derived from the Spanish *mesteño* meaning 'stranger' or 'stray animal'. Mustangs are found fending completely for themselves in areas such as the Granite Range of north-west Nevada, the Red Desert of south-west Wyoming, the Grand Canyon of Arizona, the Pryor Mountains of Montana, Death Valley in California, the Douglas Mountains of Colorado and in southern New Mexico. They are descended from escapees of the horses of Spanish Conquistadors brought over in the 16th century. For many years they provided good

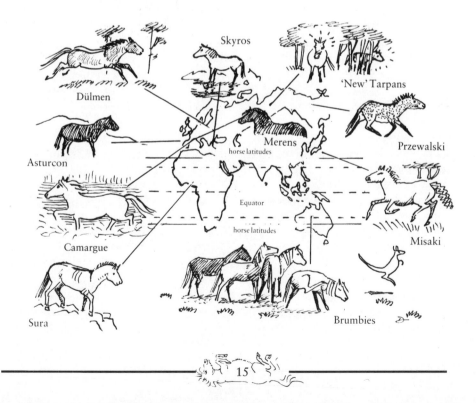

stock for ranchers and also for the army at home and abroad. As the use of the horse declined, their fate was to turn into dogmeat, resulting in a rapid decline in their numbers (to a mere 20,000!). This trade officially ceased in 1971, and since then the population has increased dramatically, to the extent that many ranchers consider them to be major pests because they are believed to compete with domestic stock for resources. They are generally small horses at around 14.2-15 hands (145-150 cm), and come in all colours.

There are three other well known North American feral populations which live in very different conditions to the Mustangs: these are the East Coast island ponies of Sable, Assateague and Shackleford.

SABLE ISLAND
Ponies have lived on this inhospitable, windswept island off the coast of Nova Scotia probably since the 17th century. The three hundred or so individuals there today are thought to be descendants of New England horses set free over two hundred years ago. Before these arrived the island was populated with cattle and ponies which had swum ashore from shipwrecks, but it is believed that most of these were eaten by humans who also swam ashore. The island is a sand bank about twenty-two miles long and less than a mile wide. Marram and other coarse grasses predominate, and there is some heathland; there is very little shelter. The ponies are stocky and fairly small (12-13 hands, 120-130 cm) and most are dark bay or brown, often with an eel stripe down their backs. They are not managed in any way, and the island is now a protected reserve with just a few human inhabitants.

ASSATEAGUE
Between two and three hundred ponies live on this thin island which stretches for about thirty miles along the coast of Maryland and Virginia. Ponies have lived here for at least three hundred years, and there are a number of theories regarding their origin. The popular, more romantic theory is that they swam ashore from a shipwrecked Spanish galleon; alternatively they may have been put there as a food supply for passing pirates (who, incidentally, never returned). The most likely theory, however, is that they are the result of a tax dodge. Early Eastern Shore settlers are believed to have 'hidden' their assets (ponies) on the island in order to avoid the taxes due and the cost of fencing; when they needed ponies they simply rounded some up. Today the population is divided in two by a fence along the Maryland-Virginia State line. In the

south (Virginia) no more than 150 ponies are allowed, and they are all owned by the Chincoteague Volunteer Fire Company. The ponies are rounded up once a year, when most foals are weaned, and they receive regular veterinary attention. By contrast, the northern herd (Maryland), owned by the National Park Service, receives very little interference. The ponies currently in the north originate from 21 Assateague ponies put there in 1965; until the mid 1980s these ponies were left completely alone, but since then some population control has been necessary in order to prevent overgrazing. Assateague ponies are fairly small, at around 12-13 hands (120-130 cm), and come in all colours.

SHACKLEFORD BANKS
Around a hundred ponies live on this narrow (about eleven miles long and less than a mile wide), sandy island off the North Carolina coast – about two hundred miles south of Assateague. The ponies here are believed to have originated from shipwrecks, and have inhabited the island since the 16th century, since when only the fittest have survived. They are a similar type of pony to that on Assateague.

Large feral populations are also found in Australia. Like the Mustangs, these have a general name -

BRUMBIES
The first free-ranging horses arrived in Australia in 1788 when one stallion, three mares and two fillies escaped into the bush; ten years later there were 117 horses! But this was just a start. By the early 1820s there were 5,000, in 1900 over 16,000 were found for regiments joining the Boer War, and in the First World War over 121,000 were taken for military service. Today's population is much reduced; they are nearly all confined to the Northern Territory deserts and mountains, where they are regarded as pests and culled because they compete with domestic stock for food. There is another, small population in the McDonnell Ranges of Central Australia (about two hundred miles west of Alice Springs), which has existed for over sixty years, and has not been hunted for the last thirty. Brumbies are horses rather than ponies and are generally of a fairly light build. Despite their use in the past, stockmen today consider them useless – at the very best.

In New Zealand there exists a similar situation with the feral horses of-

KAIMANAWA
These horses range over some 70,000 hectares (173,000 acres) in the

Kaimanawa Ranges of North Island, New Zealand. They were first recorded in 1876, although they were known to be in the Central Plateau area in the 1840s. They originated from escapees, including Welsh and Exmoor ponies from Britain, which were then crossed with local ponies to produce a hardy, sure-footed, small horse known as the 'Comet'. Since then they have bred with larger, locally bred escapees, including some turned loose by the army, and in the 1960s an Arab was reportedly released into the area. However, the horses were not popular with local stockmen as they competed with domestic stock for resources, and by the late 1970s the population had fallen to less than two hundred, mainly because of shooting. In 1981 they were given a legal protection and since then their numbers have increased by an average of 20% per year to around 1,700 in 1993. This has resulted in overgrazing and loss of habitat in some areas and humane methods of controlling the population are being sought.

Smaller populations of ponies are found in Japan, Argentina, Brazil and Nigeria. In Japan, there is a small population of the native **Misaki** horse living in the forests and open pasture of Toimisaki on Kyushu Island. In Argentina, although many horses and ponies appear to be free-ranging, most are closely managed and many are fed during the winter, but there are some feral **Criollo** ponies still living in the Pampas region. These descendants of Andalusian horses brought over by the Spaniards are large ponies at 13.3-14.3 hands (137-147 cm) and are often coloured or spotted. The **Roraima** horses of the Serrado region of Brazil (near the border with Venezuela) are also thought to be descendants of the Spanish Conquistadors' horses. They are reputed to be so fast they can maintain speeds of up to 37 mph (60 kph) for longer than a racehorse. Protection for these horses is currently being sought as numbers are falling due to their being killed for sport and meat and cross-bred with domestic stock.

The **Sura** ponies of the Jos Plateau in northern Nigeria are similarly threatened with extinction and may already have all gone. In the 1970s a small, feral herd of these slender, sure-footed ponies existed in an area of harsh, rocky terrain 1,100-1,400 metres (3,500-4,500 feet) above sea level; it is not known whether they survive today. Their origin is unknown but their distinctive appearance suggests that they are of an old type of pony rather than one that has been 'improved' by finer breeds such as Arab or Spanish Barb. They are usually dark brown or bay, with a short, upright mane and a large head with a light nose. Their markings are particularly interesting: they have an eel stripe, often a vertical shoulder stripe, zebra stripes on the legs and some have as many as thirteen dark stripes on the ribs. They are docile and easily domesticated, and were used for riding (usually by naked tribesmen and women) and as pack animals.

The Europeans
Europe (excluding Britain) is home to relatively few ponies. The largest population and probably the best known are

THE 'WHITE HORSES' OF THE CAMARGUE
The origin of these grey (let's be correct) horses of the saltmarshes of the Rhone delta is not known, but they are believed to be from ancient Eastern stock. They have lived in the area for hundreds or possibly thousands of years, and have probably always been managed in large herds on extensive pastures – there is no evidence that they have ever been truly wild. They are sturdily built and, at up to 15 hands (150 cm), are more horses than ponies.

Many of the other European populations may not be feral but originate from native stock. This is probably true for the **Asturcon** pony: a small, strong pony measuring up to 12.2 hands (125 cm), black or brown in colour, which has lived in the Asturias of northern Spain for over 2,000 years. In Germany, the **Dülmen** pony is also believed to be native, and since the 14th century a small population has run on a two-hundred-hectare reserve of moors and forest on the Duke of Croy's Estate at Meerfelder Bruch in the Westphalian Munsterland (north-west Germany). It is a medium-sized pony at around 13 hands (130 cm) and, although colours vary, most have an eel stripe down their backs and some have zebra stripes on the legs. These ponies are managed and rounded up once a year when any unwanted individuals, usually colts, are removed and sold. The **Skyros** pony is believed to be native of the Greek island of that name. It is a very small pony at 9-11 hands (90-110 cm) and is said to resemble the Tarpan – although its mane is long. There are a few **'New' Tarpans** living in the forests of the Mazurian Lake district of north-east Poland. A final small population worthy of mention here is the **Merens** pony which lives in the French Pyrenees. This is a heavy type of pony, probably descended from large, German Friesian horses.

The British

Ponies of Britain.

Britain has a remarkably large number of and diversity of native pony breeds and types for its size. Nine native breeds are usually recognized: Dartmoor, Exmoor, New Forest, Welsh (which come in three basic types – the small Welsh Mountain, the larger Welsh Pony and heavier Welsh Cobs), Dales, Fell, Highland, Shetland and Connemara; other breeds and types of ponies such as Eriskay and Lundy may also be included in this list. Not all of these breeds and types have free-ranging populations today.

Why there are so many is open to speculation. Some say that the climate is particularly suitable for ponies – plenty of rain and not too hot and not too cold; but the same could be said for much of Europe and North America. Perhaps the reasons are more sociological. Throughout history, horses have been closely linked to the lives of the British people: for transport, work – both in agriculture and in industry – and more recently for pleasure.

There are many theories about where they all came from; the most likely, and probably the most popular, is that the majority of British breeds originated from ponies that had been displaced from their northern, tundra habitats by ice as it flowed from North America and across Britain to Europe during the last Ice Age. The south of England was not covered by ice and provided the ponies with an area of tundra plains that they could colonize. Pony bones about 130,000 years old have been found in cliffs on the south coast at Brighton, where ponies grazed with mammoth, woolly rhinoceros, bison and red deer, and other, younger (12,000-year-old) remains have been found in the Mendips. The bones of two distinct sizes of pony were found: a small 'mountain pony' and a larger 'steppe horse'. As the ice retreated north, some pony populations moved up with it and colonized other parts of the country. Over the next 5-6,000 years, Britain became warmer and wetter with more lush and tall vegetation. The steppe horses appear to have died out around this time (about 7,000 years ago), probably because they could not adapt to the loss of open plains, but the mountain ponies survived and they are believed to be the ancestors of our native ponies. They are usually referred to as 'British Hill' or 'Celtic' ponies. Studies of the remains of these ancient ponies, in particular their jaws, teeth and limb bones, suggest that they were similar in size and conformation to the Exmoor pony of today (see below). Over the years, these ponies would have diversified in appearance as they evolved to fit their local environments, but the most significant modifications would have occurred relatively recently as man selected the types that best fitted his needs, so creating the breeds we know today. Man continues to breed ponies selectively and, sadly, within some breeds, the original type and the hardiness that went with it has been lost. There are no ponies in Britain that are not managed in some way by man and they are all owned – often by local people with common rights attached to their properties.

The free-rangers
There are a number of populations in Britain which by and large fend for themselves all year. They are allowed to breed at will and to roam relatively unrestricted over what is usually common land, although the

release of stallions and the weaning of foals is usually controlled.

Most are rounded up at least once a year – but not necessarily all ponies are caught (see Ponies and people section). The largest populations are found on Dartmoor (Devon), in the New Forest (Hampshire), on the Gower Peninsula and Welsh hills (South/Mid Wales) and on Exmoor (Somerset/north Devon). These are described below together with other, smaller populations.

DARTMOOR

About 5,000 ponies (fewer in winter) range freely on some 365 square miles of granite moorland 500-700 metres (1,500-2,000 feet) above sea level in south Devon. The soil is thin, acidic, and consequently poor and unproductive, except in the lowland valleys. The ponies have virtually unrestricted access to the whole moor, although there are some fenced commons around the edge. They share the area with numerous sheep and cattle. Sad to say, most of the ponies seen on Dartmoor (and there is usually a plentiful supply around the most popular car parks) are not true Dartmoor ponies. There have been a number of introductions to the breed, especially Shetland – dating back to the days of pit ponies when smaller ponies were particularly useful. It is probably the effect of the Shetland that has resulted in many of the ponies on the moor being coloured (piebald, skewbald or a mixture of both); coloured ponies are not eligible for registration as Dartmoor ponies, but apparently they can fetch good prices at sales. Most registered Dartmoor ponies are now bred and reared on studs in the area, but moves have been made recently to improve the quality and hardiness of ponies on the moor. In 1988 the Dartmoor Moorland Scheme was set up; under this scheme, which is overseen and funded by the Dartmoor Pony Society, the National Park Authority, the Duchy of Cornwall and the Ministry of Agriculture, ponies selected as being true to the Dartmoor type, both in appearance and hardiness, are kept and bred in a few enclosed areas of high, open moorland called 'Newtakes'. This was followed in 1989 by the Dartmoor Pony Support Scheme, funded by the National Park Authority, which pays a premium to owners of moorland herds of ponies deemed to resemble the original type. Until recently, there was no control on the type of stallion released, but now in some areas the release of coloured or particularly large stallions is being restricted. A true Dartmoor pony is small, at no more than 12.2 hands (125 cm), and most are bay, brown or black.

NEW FOREST

Some 3,000 ponies (decreasing to around 2,000 in winter) range freely over about 50,000 acres of lowland wet and dry heathland and acid grassland. The soil is acidic and poor with a low productivity, except in the river flood plains. The name 'Forest' has nothing to do with trees but derives from its old meaning of 'hunting area' – only about 18% of the New Forest is deciduous, non-plantation woodland. The ponies share the area with cattle, five species of deer – although these are also able to use a further 8,700 hectares (21,500 acres) of enclosed woodland plantation – about eight donkeys, a few sheep in certain areas and pigs in the autumn. Any unshod pony mare or gelding can be released onto the Forest, upon payment of a nominal fee, but the release of stallions is strictly controlled. Stallions must be registered in the New Forest Studbook and to have passed veterinary and Breed Society inspections at two, three and five years of age. In addition, from 1992-3, stallions have had to spend the winter of their fifth year living unaided on the Forest; if they do not maintain good body condition during this time, they are not allowed to continue running on the Forest, although they are still accepted as stud stallions. The majority of ponies running on the Forest today are registered New Forest but it is a breed that has undergone many 'improvements' over the years, usually in response to market forces at the time. Just about all the other British native breeds, together with Arab, Thoroughbred and Hackney, have been introduced at some time in the pony's history. Although there have been no further introductions since the 1930s, not surprisingly today's pony is quite variable in its conformation and temperament. They come in a wide range of sizes from about 12 hands up to 14.2 (120-145 cm), and although most ponies are bay, chestnut or grey, all other colours occur, but piebald and skewbald ponies are not eligible for registration. The New Forest pony is a good example of how the original pony, with its naturally evolved qualities of hardiness and strength, can be lost through man's well meaning intervention.

WELSH

Ponies have lived on the Welsh hills and mountains for at least 2,000 years. Many ponies still remain, but most do not now fend for themselves all year. Welsh Mountain ponies, like many of our native breeds, were 'improved' by Arab stallions released onto the hills in the middle of the 19th century. Subsequent ponies were perhaps 'prettier' but they paid the price in a loss of hardiness. Many are now bred on lowland studs. Before the Arabs were introduced, most of the ponies were dark

Welsh ponies at Hay Bluff.

in colour with few white facial or leg markings and the hair of their coats, manes and tails was coarse and provided good protection from the elements. The Arabs are thought to have introduced greys and chestnuts, and white leg and face markings. Many of the mares and nearly all of the stallions that are free-ranging today are registered Welsh Mountain (section A) ponies (or eligible for registration). Most are of the 'older' type of pony similar to the sort that would have preceded the Arab introduction; it is unlikely that the showier, lighter weight types of the lowlands could survive on the hill all year. Some cross-breds are also turned out, together with a few Shetlands in some areas. The ponies share the exposed, moorland terrain of the hills and mountains of south and mid-Wales with sheep and a few cattle, but in many areas the number of ponies turned out is declining. In the Brecon Beacons, for example, two to three hundred ponies could be found on the commons fifteen years ago; today you would be lucky to find fifty. Many of the commoners have given up in this area because the ponies were being injured or killed on busy roads. The largest single population of ponies that fend for themselves in Wales is not found on the hills but on the Gower peninsula in South Wales. This is a coastal area of patches of common land consisting of saltmarshes, sand dunes and acid grassland and heathland. It is believed to have been grazed by ponies for over a thousand years. Until 1967 the ponies shared the area with sheep, but now only rabbits feed alongside the ponies. The Gower is home to about five hundred ponies of somewhat mixed ancestry, including pit ponies, Welsh Cobs, Welsh Mountain ponies and ponies 'improved' by Arab and Thoroughbred blood. However, stallions released today have to be registered Welsh Mountain (Welsh Section A) and are inspected annually by the Gower Welsh Mountain Improvement Society. The Gower ponies are of a mixed appearance from small and fine boned to heavy, taller and cob-like. All colours are found, with bays and greys being most common; piebalds and skewbalds are rare and not eligible for registration in the Welsh Pony and Cob Society Stud Book. Welsh Mountain ponies are still being used as pit ponies in some of the small, private collieries of South Wales.

EXMOOR
About 150 pure bred ponies and a smaller, variable number of cross-bred ponies live all year on about 17,000 hectares (42,000 acres) of moorland. Exmoor lies on Old Red sandstone and the soil, although acidic, is generally more productive than that of Dartmoor, for example. The area is very exposed to strong winds from the Bristol Channel and, apart from the deep valleys, or 'coombes', there is little shelter. Until the early 1800s Exmoor was a Royal Forest (like the New Forest, it was a place for hunting) and the ponies roamed freely throughout the area. In 1818 Exmoor ceased to be a Royal Forest, areas were enclosed and the free movement of the ponies was, and still is, restricted by fences. The ponies share the moor with sheep, cattle and red deer. Exmoor ponies have lived on the moor for thousands of years and, probably because of the relative remoteness of the area, compared with the other British breeds, have suffered little interference from man. Today's ponies are considered to be relatively pure-bred, and all are closely inspected (literally with a fine tooth comb!) before being passed to enter the Stud Book; any white hairs (except for injury scars) and they cannot be registered. Stallions undergo even greater scrutiny and any doubts about their

health or conformation result in their rejection (and, inevitably, the gelding knife). As a result of these inspections the Exmoor breed is very uniform in appearance. They are small, very sturdy ponies; mares can be up to 12.2 hands (125 cm) and stallions to 12.3 hands (127 cm). They range in colour from a dark dun through bay to brown and all have an oatmeal ('mealy') coloured muzzle and ring round the eye (this uniformity has caused considerable problems in the past to the field biologist wishing to identify individuals – paint has been tried to give ponies individual marks for identification but it does not stick). The Exmoor pony is listed as 'critical' by the Rare Breeds Survival Trust; at the last count there were only about 800 left in the world.

For the other breeds and types only small free-ranging populations remain today and these are described below. Unfortunately there are no remaining free-ranging groups of Dales ponies.

FELL
There is a handful of Fell ponies living in a semi-wild state on the Cumbrian moors, sometimes referred to as Pennine Ponies or Fell-Galloways; some believe that these large, sturdy ponies may have originated from the larger steppe horse (although there is no hard evidence for this) which managed to survive in the area and was later enlarged by

Highland ponies on the island of Rhum.

the Romans. Today's Fell pony measures up to 14 hands (140 cm), and most are black or brown, with some bays and greys.

HIGHLAND

There is a small herd of Highland ponies living on the Isle of Rhum – although purists say that these are not true Highland but small Rhum ponies. As with the Fell, it has been suggested that the Highland (and Rhum) pony probably originated from the larger type of Celtic pony. It is a large, strong pony up to 14.2 hands (145 cm), usually grey or dun – of which there are a range of shades from mouse to yellow dun – usually with an eel stripe along the spine and sometimes zebra marks on the legs; bays and browns occur but are less common.

SHETLAND

The majority of Shetland ponies on the Shetland Islands are now kept and bred in fenced 'parks' around crofts, but there are some living on common land or 'scattalds'. In the nineteenth century ponies were left completely to their own devices on the scattalds, but this is rarely the case today. The wet and windswept nature of the Shetland Islands has

Shetland ponies.

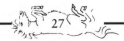

Connemara mare and foal.

been the major factor shaping the small, hairy, hardy Shetland which is known to have inhabited the area for at least 2,500 years. They measure up to 10.2 hands (105 cm) and come in all colours, with piebald and skewbald being common.

ERISKAY
This is an old breed said to be the last survivor of the native ponies of the Hebrides. There are a few Eriskays free-living on the Ochils (between the Forth and Tay valleys, Perthshire) and on Holy Island, Arran – although the island has recently been sold and it is not yet known under what conditions the ponies are to be kept in the future. Eriskays are grey and at 12-13 hands (120-130 cm) are stocky, small to medium sized ponies – apparently they were selectively bred for small size so that they were easier for women to manage. Eriskays have recently been listed as 'endangered' by the Rare Breeds Survival Trust.

There are two other British ponies that are not directly descended from native stock: these are the Connemara and the Lundy pony.

CONNEMARA
There are now only a few Connemaras free ranging on the sides of

mountains in Connemara, western Ireland. It is a mountainous, boggy region with grassy valleys, located to the west of Loughs Corrib and Mask close to the Atlantic and Galway Bay coasts. Connemaras are not true native ponies, although there have probably been ponies living in the area since the fourth century BC; the first ponies are thought to have come with the Celts from the Alps and the valleys of the Danube. Spanish horses may have been introduced at some time, together with Andalusians from shipwrecks. In addition, Arab blood was introduced until the middle of the last century. Connemaras are one of the larger types of British ponies, most are between 13 and 14 hands (130-140 cm); grey is the most common colour, but there are also blacks, browns, bays and chestnuts; sadly dun, the original colour of these ponies, is now very scarce.

LUNDY

There are a few ponies fending for themselves on this small island in the Bristol Channel, but there is much exchange with stock kept on the mainland in south-west England. Unlike all the other British ponies, the Lundy is not an ancient breed but a product of twentieth-century breeding from a stock of New Forest and Welsh Mountain, followed by later additions of Welsh, New Forest and Connemara. Some British pony enthusiasts and experts do not yet regard the Lundy pony as a breed in its own right, although there is a set of breed standards, a Stud Book and a breed society. Lundy ponies measure between 13 and 14 hands, and the preferred colour is dun, although roan, bay, palomino and dark liver chestnut are allowed.

Free-ranging horses and ponies are found in many parts of the world, and nearly all owe their present-day existence to European influence and European stock. Populations in the Americas and Australasia are relatively recent, following in the wake of European colonists. By contrast, the majority of populations in Britain and Europe are ancient; some are thousands of years old. I have been fortunate in spending a number of years studying the ponies in the New Forest, together with a shorter time with those on Exmoor and Dartmoor. Since this is where my 'experience' lies, this book will draw many of its examples from these populations. I hope enthusiasts of the other populations will not feel offended by my bias.

Special equipment

With only two coats, a pony's wardrobe is somewhat limited.

Ponies are gregarious animals which live predominantly in open areas and spend most of their lives grazing and browsing. They are able to live in a wide range of environments varying from deserts to marshes, from small, sandy windswept islands to mountains, often tolerating extremes of temperature and shortages of food and water. They have always been the hunted rather than the hunter, and it is only recently that for most the threat of attack from predators such as wolves, large cats and man no longer exists – unlike their striped relatives in Africa. Old habits die hard, however, and the detection and avoidance of predators is of equal but conflicting importance as the need to feed. Over the millions of years of evolution ponies have become very well equipped to cope with this kind of lifestyle. Their bodywork is well designed for protection from the elements, they have an efficient food processing machinery, an alert early warning system and powerful one-horsepower engine for rapid getaway.

Environmental protection

A pony's coat is its physical means of protection from the elements; it must be waterproof and cold or warm at the appropriate time of the year. With only two coats for the whole year, a pony's wardrobe is somewhat limited, but in the successful pony these are well designed for the job. The winter coat is the more important for survival, although a long mane, forelock and tail reduce attack and aggravation by flies in summer. The winter coat begins to grow in late August and, when complete, consists of two layers: an undercoat of fine, springy, short hairs (usually up to 4 cm/1½ inches long) and an overcoat of longer, coarse, 'guard' hairs. The coat is well supplied with an oily substance called 'sebum' (secreted by the sebaceous glands in the skin) which helps with insulation and reduces the amount of water retained by the hair. More insulation is gained by the involuntary contraction of bundles of muscle fibres in the skin which make each hair stand up, so trapping more air in the coat and increasing heat retention. The sight of ponies with unmelted snow on their backs confirms that this coat provides excellent insulation. The shedding of the winter coat begins in early March, first from the limbs and underparts, and then from the back. The summer coat consists of short, fine hairs and, in adults, is usually complete by the end of May, although a cold, wet spring may delay this. Most foals are born in the summer and arrive with a short, springy coat. If born late, they arrive well prepared for the weather with a much thicker coat, nearer to the winter type of an older foal. As a rule, old and young ponies and those in poor body condition (excessively thin) keep their winter coats for longer. These are the groups of ponies that need to conserve most energy: young ponies have to find extra energy for growth and develop-

The coat provides excellent insulation.

ment, older ponies need more to keep warm and alive, and those in poor condition need a surplus of energy in order to make up their body reserves. Wearing a warm coat which retains body heat efficiently leaves more energy available for other purposes.

The way the coat lies is as important as its composition. A glance at any horse reveals that the hairs do not all lie in the same direction (considering the shape of a horse this would be impossible anyway). The direction in which the hair lies directs the flow of rainwater off the coat; if this does not work then the pony ends up with wet, and consequently cold, patches, just as if there were holes in the coat. The points at which hairs meet are called whorls or vortices; their position is unique to each individual – like equine fingerprints. The vortices that are probably most important to survival lie on each side of the body in front of the pelvis; for the most efficient shedding of water, they should run vertically from just below the point of the hip to the flank in front of the thigh, and the hairs should lie so that water cannot run down to the inside of the thigh where the coat is very thin and fine. Other rain-shedding features include long hairs under the chin and down the legs, the mane, the forelock, and a tail set low down the rump to keep the hairless anal and genital regions warm. Many ponies have a particularly low set on tail, at the top of which is a fan of tail hair or 'snow chute', the purpose of which needs no explanation. This feature is particularly noticeable in Exmoor ponies.

Like a human, a pony can regulate its body temperature further by shivering when it is cold – the contraction of the muscles involved produces heat – and when it is too hot it is able to sweat from all parts of the body except the legs. The nose helps to conserve heat by warming up

The coat lies in such a way that water is directed off it.

the air that a pony breathes in before it reaches its lungs. Ponies cannot breathe through their mouths, and cold air taken in through their large, broad nostrils is warmed as it passes along long nasal passages lined with mucous membranes and well supplied with blood.

Shedding the coat also helps other animals.

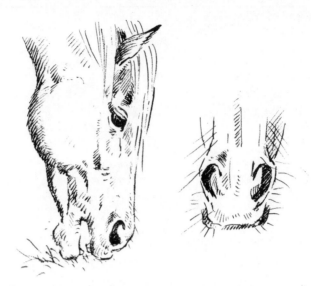

The first points of contact with food are the ponies' sensitive whiskers and nose, then its teeth.

Food processing

The first point of contact between a pony and its meal, after its sensitive nose, whiskers and lips have selected what is to be eaten, is the teeth, which must cope with a wide range of foods (see pp. 58-60). They must function efficiently if the digestive processes which follow are to be efficient. Like most herbivores ponies have incisors at the front of the jaw for biting, and premolars with complex surfaces further back for grinding and chewing. The permanent (adult) teeth are high crowned and have veins of tough enamel running down through them as well as round the edge – so providing a good, rough grinding surface. They continue to grow through life, although the rate of wear is often greater than the rate of growth. Horses have incisors on both upper and lower jaws (six on each), unlike many of the other ungulates; cattle, sheep and deer, for example, only have incisors on the lower jaw – the upper jaw is a bony pad. Adult ponies have twelve or fourteen premolars and molars in the upper jaw and twelve in the lower. Between the premolars and the incisors is a gap, the diastema, which is used to store bitten off food before it is ground up by the premolars and molars. Canine teeth, used for piercing prey in the carnivores, are only found in adult male horses, although a vestigial tooth may be found in the jaw of mares. It is unclear why males have retained their canine teeth, but they could be used in

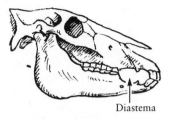

Skull, showing diastema.

Diastema

fighting to damage the tendons of an opponent's lower leg.

The food that a free-ranging pony's teeth are expected to deal with is often very coarse and woody (see pp. 58-60), so a large, strong jaw, and the large head that inevitably goes with it, are essential. Unfortunately most show rings do not appreciate ponies with large, strong heads and within some breeds this feature has been discouraged and subsequently lost, together with the ability to tackle large quantities of very tough, coarse food.

Tooth troubles

Without a good set of biters and chewers ponies cannot be expected to thrive. Problems with teeth are often linked to a pony's age. Young ponies, like children, often have temporary gaps when their milk teeth are being replaced by the permanent adult teeth; this can be a particular problem for two- to three-year-olds which may be unable to bite effectively whilst their front four incisors are being replaced. Old ponies' teeth are frequently badly worn or loose as a result of years of grazing on short grass on sandy soil and browsing coarse vegetation; in many cases they are unable to bite effectively because the upper and lower incisors no longer meet. Irregularly

and excessively worn and excessively sharp molars are also common problems for these ponies. They cannot chew properly and often suffer much discomfort if the sharp edges of the molars lacerate the inside of the cheeks. In the domestic situation this is usually prevented by regular rasping of the molars (usually by a vet or farrier) but, not surprisingly, the rasping of free-ranging ponies' teeth is something of a rarity.

As a result of this excessive wear, it is difficult to estimate accurately the age of a pony by examining its teeth for shape and wear. It is possible for free-ranging ponies aged up to five years, whilst the milk teeth are being replaced (although

R·L·TUSK
DENTIST

"M' molars are too sharp"

"M' teeth are too small"

"– or mine don't meet"

examining the teeth of most free-ranging ponies is not a practice I would recommend), but older ponies' teeth do not necessarily conform to the standards for domestic horses which normally eat less abrasive food.

By the end of its first year a pony has six milk (temporary) incisor teeth in each jaw, at around 2¹/₂ years the central pairs fall out and are replaced by adult teeth, at about 3¹/₂ years all four central teeth have been replaced and between 4 and 5 years of age the outer ('corner') incisors are replaced.

Some ponies experience a different kind of problem in which their teeth are not in proportion to their jaws: large teeth in shallow jaws, small teeth in deep jaws and sometimes large incisors and small molars (or vice versa) in the same jaw. This is believed to be the outcome of the crossing of horses such as Arabs, which have shallow jaws and small teeth, with Celtic or native types of ponies, which have large teeth in deep jaws. Such misfits can lead to badly aligned or irregular teeth, premature loosening, uneven wear and two teeth occupying the same socket.

Once the food has been bitten off and ground up, ponies are well equipped for efficient further processing. They have a long gut of about thirty metres (varying with size and type of pony), which includes one, small stomach – unlike ruminants such as cattle, sheep and deer which have four. A major constituent of any vegetarian diet is cellulose, which is present in the cell walls of all vegetable matter. Cellulose needs special bacteria in order to be digested; in ruminants these bacteria are present in the rumen, the first stomach, but in horses they are found further down the gut in the caecum, a long, sack-like structure at the junction of the small and large intestine. A ruminant has to stop feeding in order to chew the partially digested food (cud) after it has been through the

Ponies can eat – continuously.

rumen; ponies do not have to do this, and consequently they can eat almost continuously, relying more on quantity than quality of food to obtain sufficient nutrition. This ability of ponies to eat large quantities is probably one of the secrets of their success. They can make the best of poor quality food, provided that there is plenty of it. Such a bulk intake of food does not, however, do much for a pony's figure!

Early warning system
The ears, eyes and nose of a pony are designed to detect danger long before it arrives.

Ears: ponies can usually tell the direction of a sound before they can see the source. This is because each ear is controlled by ten muscles and can move independently in almost any direction. Ponies can hear sounds of a wider and higher range of frequencies than humans (55 hertz – 33.5 kilohertz compared with a humans' 29 hertz – 19 kilohertz), and their best range of hearing is between 1 and 16 kilohertz (man's is 500 hertz-8 kilohertz). Like humans, however, ponies lose sensitivity to the higher frequencies as they grow older. It is believed that stallions have better hearing than geldings or mares. The reason for this is not certain but one theory is that stallions, which are usually the most vigilant members of a pony group (see page 51), need superior hearing to detect predators and, perhaps, potential competitors.

Eyes: the position of a pony's eyes on its head provides it with a wide field of vision. When the head is raised, the only blind spots are a strip from the ears, down the back of the neck, back and directly behind the hind-quarters, and on the ground from the forelegs to about a metre in front of the head. With only slight movements of the head, the pony can see all around. Each eye has a field of vision of up to 215°, most of which is monocular (two-dimensional), so that a pony can literally see two things at once. In front of the head, these fields of vision overlap and provide 60-70° of binocular (three-dimensional) vision. This relatively small area of binocular vision allows the horse to detect movement at great distance but, unlike humans which have a much wider binocular field of vision of about 130°, a pony is not very good at judging distances. The field of view is affected by the shape and position of the head, and the size of the eye and jaw. Large eyes that are wide apart increase the field of view, and wide and deep jaws decrease the view below the head. Not much is known about ponies' focusing abilities, but they may be a little 'long-sighted' as they are able to focus continuously from about a metre in front but objects closer than this are thought to appear blurred.

We noted earlier how the need to feed was potentially in conflict with the need to be watchful and flee danger; to help in this a pony's retina (the light receptive membrane in the eye) is inclined so that the horse can see around without having to raise its head and stop eating.

Can ponies see in the dark? Can they see colours? The answers to these questions are not fully known. Ponies certainly see much better in the dark than humans, and there is evidence that they can see colour, although their colour vision is not believed to be as good as ours. Ponies can distinguish between a colour and a grey of equal intensity; studies of the colour sensitive cones on the retina suggest that ponies are relatively insensitive to red, but can discriminate well between shades of blue and between shades of green. This supports results from other tests which

A pony's blind spots when standing still.

Ponies can see around themselves without having to stop eating.

suggest that ponies can see blue, and are able to differentiate between shades of yellow and green, but they cannot distinguish red from blue.

Nose: ponies are known to have an excellent sense of smell but relatively little is understood about the way in which it works. Smell is used in the identification of food, locations and other individuals. Specific uses of smell will be covered in more detail later on (see pages 56, 68 and 72).

Ponies don't judge distance very well.

Why do ponies curl up their upper lips?

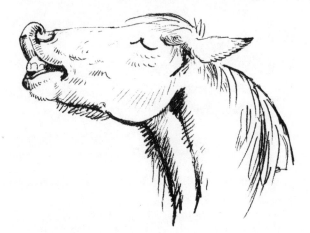

Flehmen.

Do they like making faces? Are they especially proud of their teeth?

This curious reaction is particularly common in stallions when sniffing dung and urine, and during sexual encounters when sniffing the mare. It is called 'flehmen' (pronounced 'flay-men'). This is a German word for which there is no exact English translation. The correct use of the word is problematic, and I shall adopt the practice of the latest edition of the Encyclopaedia Britannica *which says that the horse 'exhibits*

flehmen'. The action of curling up the lip is believed to activate extra olfactory (smelling) receptors located in the nose in the Vomeronasal (Jacobsen's) organ. These receptors are believed to be particularly responsive to social and sexual smells, although, especially in domestic horses, flehmen is sometimes exhibited after feeding. My own mare frequently exhibited flehmen after receiving a carrot or similar titbit – whether she found carrots and the like particularly sexy I shall never know.

The frog – a shock absorber and anti-slip device.

The getaway

Having detected danger and decided that escape is the best strategy, the pony's long legs, flexible joints, powerful muscles, tendons and ligaments and its four hard 'toes' are put into action. The power needed for acceleration lies in the muscles of its hindquarters. The upper part of the leg is short, powerful and well muscled and the lower leg is long, slender, without muscle but with strong ligaments and tendons which act as springs and shock absorbers. The hoof is hard and compact, allowing the pony to move quickly over firm ground, and it also features a shock absorber and anti-slip device, the frog (so-called because it is thought to look like one). This is an elastic, V-shaped mass of tissue on the sole of the hoof, a remnant of a foot pad. Its elastic structure cushions the impact with the ground for the hoof and leg, and its wedge shape, with the broad end at the back of the hoof and the point half to two-thirds of the way forwards, provides grip. The sole of the hoof is in fact quite soft, but because of the the protection afforded by the frog and the tough, keratinized outer layer of the hoof, it does not normally make hard contact with the ground; if it does, it can become damaged or bruised on sharp, irregular surfaces.

There are four gaits: walk, trot, canter and gallop. The way in which these gaits are used is very similar to the gears on a car or bicycle; ponies change up a gait, for example from trot to canter, when the energy required to stay in the lower gait, the trot, is greater than would be required to maintain the same or greater speed in canter.

The fastest horses can reach speeds of up to 43 mph (65 kph) but this is not sustainable over a long distance and highly unlikely in the average free-ranging pony. During the initial stages of a fast sprint a pony can hold its breath for about thirty seconds, which allows it to make a very rapid initial getaway without having the added complication of breathing; but after this period the rate of air intake usually has to increase in order to make up the oxygen debt.

A natural group

We usually think of horses, zebras and the like as living in large social groups but in fact some members of the horse family are quite anti-social. The asses of Africa and Asia (including the feral donkey) and Grevy's zebras go through life without maintaining any long-lasting bonds between individuals. They live in temporary, loose groups and their longest lasting relationships (between mother and offspring) do not last for more than two years. During the breeding season, a stallion of these species defends a permanent territory of at least 3½ square miles (10 square km) in which only he can cover the mares that enter. He may keep the same territory for years, but leave for a while during a drought.

By contrast, the mountain and plains zebra and unmanaged feral horses are far more sociable. They live in permanent, family groups with a single adult male and do not defend a territory. These groups are called harems, or 'bands' in America, and usually consist of a single male with up to six females and their young. In some areas, such as Sable Island (Nova Scotia), one male may have a harem of up to twenty females. The harem lives within a given area or 'home range', and within a population (see Glossary) home ranges of different groups overlap considerably. Home ranges differ from territories in that they are not defended. Their size is highly variable and depends on the local environment and the resources it offers, but will always include a main feeding site, such as a grassland plain, a water supply, and an area of shelter and shade.

The harem.

American Wild Horse Band.

Males and females are born in roughly equal numbers. The harem type of social organization inevitably leads to a number of surplus males. These are usually young males that were driven out of their father's harem when they began to show too much interest in his mares, and have yet to form their own harem, and old stallions who have been deposed by younger, fitter horses. These unattached males form 'bachelor groups' or, as they are aptly called in North America, 'rowdy gangs'; the size of these groups is usually between two and eight individuals but occasionally they are larger. These all-male groups usually occupy smaller, lower quality home ranges than those of the harems. Within groups the young males often 'practise' being stallions by play-fighting – a less serious form of adult fighting that includes more biting of the face – mounting other males (which can cause a fight) and adopting high-stepping and dunging postures (see page 55).

There are exceptions to every rule. Where food, water and shelter are limited, or conditions particularly harsh, horses adopt different social structures and in some cases will defend territories, as on Shackleford Island off the coast of North Carolina. This is a long, thin island, two-thirds of which is very flat and made up of three vegetation zones. The horses need to use all three zones to survive, and so each stallion defends a territory for his harem which includes a portion of each zone.

In other locations, groups with more than one stallion have been recorded, notably in areas where food and water are scarce, such as in

Rowdy gang.

the Red Desert (north-west Wyoming) and in the McDonnell Ranges (central Australia). By joining forces, these groups become bigger and the individuals within benefit because a large group can out-compete smaller groups for resources. One stallion is usually dominant over the other; he benefits because he has access to more mares, even though he may have to share some of them, and he has a subordinate stallion to assist him in aggressive encounters between groups. The subordinate stallion also gains from this arrangement because he is with a potentially more successful group and may achieve some matings – which he otherwise probably would not.

Leaving home
A pony is unlikely to remain in the same group for life. As mentioned earlier, colts are soon pushed out of the harem once their attitude towards the mares poses any threat to the stallion. Some colts are earlier developers than others and may be rejected in their second year; others may be tolerated for longer by the stallion, particularly if they help to drive away intruders. Fillies usually stay with their dams for about three years; they may then leave the harem of their own will, they may be pushed out by their sire, or be stolen by a neighbouring stallion – often a young male forming his first harem. This dispersal of the young has probably evolved to reduce inbreeding. On Assateague island, young ponies sometimes stay together after leaving the natal group and form small, mixed sex bands. Although there is some sexual activity between these individuals, no foals are born and it is thought that they are probably together through the need for companionship (see page 51) rather than reproduction. These individuals eventually become members of harems or bachelor groups.

There is little or no sexual interest or activity between parents and offspring or between siblings. If young ponies do not leave their natal group, their chances of breeding are reduced unless the stallion changes.

An unnatural group

The natural social order works very well until man enters the scene and starts to 'manage'. In Britain today there are no truly unmanaged populations, and the social organization that exists in our free-ranging populations is distorted from that of the more 'wild' Mustangs of North America or the Brumbies of Australia.

In Britain, 'management' consists mainly of the removal of most foals (especially colts) for sale at around four months of age, and the restriction of the number of stallions released. In the Gower all colt foals are removed by the time they are a year old. It is the management of stallions that particularly affects social organization. Instead of the natural 1:1 male to female ratio, an unnaturally small number of stallions is allowed to run with the mares; this ranges from about one stallion to 13 mares on Exmoor, 1:30 in the New Forest, and an extreme 1:60 has at times been the case on the Gower peninsula. Moreover in the Gower it is common for all stallions to be removed for the winter, usually for riding; many are removed from the Welsh hills, and in the New Forest about a third are removed.

Having disrupted the sex ratio, man must 'manage' further in order to permit breeding and prevent inbreeding. For example, in the Gower, where only about six stallions are released, it is unlikely that they would be able to encounter, let alone cover, all the sexually mature mares in the area. In order to improve the mares' chances of breeding, stallions have in the past been moved round between the commons. In the New Forest, it is deemed necessary to move a stallion to a different area every four to five years in order to prevent inbreeding. This is often easier said than done since many stallions object to being moved and expend a lot of time and energy returning to their former ranges, sometimes resulting in injury or death from crossing roads or unknown territory. The scheme has also been known to backfire when stallions have been inadvertently moved to an area where their father or other close relation has ranged.

Management of stallions may serve to reduce the amount of aggression and fighting in these areas but it also disrupts the natural social order I have described: the harem, avoidance of inbreeding, the natural selection of stallions through competition, and the existence of bachelor groups. The basic social structure in the Gower and the New Forest is of small groups of two or three mares and offspring, which may form larger,

Dartmoor ponies at Saddle Tor.

temporary groups in the breeding season. In the New Forest, exceptions are found where the stallion is out all year and has not been, or will not be moved; when this happens, there exists a harem type of organization in which the stallion is accompanied by a group of up to five or six 'core' mares and offspring, and these are joined by more mares in the summer. Within such a group, as with the unmanaged ponies, fillies will leave for a neighbouring group at about three years of age. A similar situation exists on Exmoor and Dartmoor where most stallions are out all year, and their relocation is generally less frequent here; and groups of the same adults generally stay together until the resident stallion is removed or dies.

Variety is not the spice of life?

Changing the sex ratio and moving stallions may have other consequences besides an unnatural social organization. Despite very harsh environmental conditions experienced by some unmanaged populations – such as deep snow and gales on Sable Island, drought and high temperatures in the Red Desert – the production of foals is often considerably higher than that in the managed populations of Britain. For exam-

ple, around 80% of Sable Island mares produce foals each year, whereas only 40-50% foal in the New Forest (although mortality of foals is lower there). This may be because there are relatively few stallions available to cover mares in the New Forest, but it also suggests that removing or changing a stallion contributes to the relatively low production of foals by managed populations. In the Great Basin, Colorado, the number of mares foaling decreased markedly after the death and subsequent replacement of a long-standing stallion.

Murder?

In some populations, a stallion new to a group has been known to kill the foals of his predecessor. This is usually achieved by physically attacking the foals, but it has been suggested that it may also come about by causing the pregnant mare to abort through forced copulation. After aborting, the mare comes into season and is receptive to the new stallion. Whatever the method, the outcome of this behaviour is to increase the new stallion's genetic influence on the population and reduce that of his predecessor.

Who's who within the group

Girls on top

Within a harem or group of any population (I prefer to call the 'harem' of a managed population a group), despite any disruption that man's interference causes, the individuals keep themselves in order and maintain a dominance hierarchy (pecking order) in which the stallion is not necessarily dominant. A mare's position in the hierarchy is related more to her individual personality than to physical features such as size. I have known some small but aggressive individuals with sharp heels who will take on and displace much larger ponies. Age also plays a major part. Young ponies aged less than four years are usually subordinate and sometimes very old ponies will 'lose rank', although in most cases they remain dominant even when they are physically less fit than their subordinates; but between these extremes personality is more important in most populations. Exceptions occur, as in the Grand Canyon for example, where the hierarchy of the mares is related to size and bigger mares dominate.

The hierarchy is generally of a linear nature, in that the most dominant mare is dominant over all below her, the second mare is dominant over all except the one above and so on. But there are individual relationships that jump out of line; in a New Forest group that I studied, a high-ranking mare, 'Apache', was subordinate to a much lower ranking mare, 'Black Strawberry', but not to those individuals ranked in between. Once a group is established, the dominance hierarchy does not change substantially from year to year unless an individual dies, leaves or is removed, although young ponies (aged up to five years) tend to move up as they mature.

Maintaining order

Ponies have two main weapons, teeth and hooves, both of which can inflict serious damage but are rarely used for this purpose. Most aggression is expressed as a threat, which carries less risk of retaliation and requires much less energy than actually making contact by biting or kicking. When it comes down to contact some mares tend to be kickers and others biters, and they use these actions if threats do not work; some individuals will even by-pass the threat stage altogether.

The purpose of a hierarchy in which each individual knows its place is to reduce aggression, and within an established group it is very rare for one

'Move out of my way.'

member to injure another. However, there are always some ponies that feel the need to reinforce their positions more than others and others that need to be reminded of it. This is particularly common between ponies of similar rank and in encounters that involve young mares or new members of the group who are trying to move up in the hierarchy.

The hierarchy is maintained by threat and submission and rarely by fighting. The mildest and the most common threat is the 'ear threat' where the ears are laid back towards the neck. If this has the desired effect and the recipient pony moves out of the way, then no further action is taken. If it is not successful the aggressor will repeat the gesture, often with increased intensity with the ears laid back on the neck, the mouth slightly open and a sharp raising of the head (a 'head threat'). If this does not work then she may threaten to bite or kick – which in most cases does the trick! Sometimes the aggressor lunges at or chases her opponent, usually threatening to bite her; this is quite a common behaviour and although it requires more energy than just threatening it carries less risk for the aggressor than actually making contact. Physical contact is a last resort.

Although a subordinate mare will usually give way to a dominant, subordinate mares frequently also respond by threatening one of their subordinates, and so a wave of aggression passes down the line, ending with the lowest ranking individuals who lead a somewhat disturbed life being pushed around by everyone else. However, when an unfamiliar mare approaches or tries to join the group, out come the teeth and heels of all ranks – even the most subordinate (who perhaps take a positive delight in being on the giving rather than receiving end!). The stranger does not know her place in the hierarchy. If she stays, then, after encounters with members of the group of all ranks she will find her place, aggression levels will fall again and the hierarchy will change to accommodate her.

'Move out of my way – or else!'

Very young members of the group, particularly foals, do not redirect aggression from an older member of the group, even to other foals. They respond to threats or uncertain encounters with an adult with what is believed to be a submissive gesture, known as 'snapping' (sometimes called 'champing'). The young pony's neck is slightly outstreched, the ears are out to the side or slightly back and it opens and closes its mouth without allowing the lips to touch whilst drawing back the corners of the mouth. Snapping does not necessarily prevent an aggressive attack but it may reduce the intensity of it. Young ponies also snap when approaching an adult – or even a cow! In the Camargue, when snapping has failed to appease a threatening adult, a foal may go down onto its knees and then roll over with its legs in the air, like a submissive dog, in order to avoid further aggression. I have not seen this or heard of it in other populations.

Why be dominant?
The dominant mare is able to do what she wants within a group. She can push her subordinates out of the way should she desire a particular food or other resource and, especially in the breeding season, she can usually be found

'Please like me.'

Allogrooming.

close to the stallion – which is probably the best place to be (see page 74). It is usually the dominant mare and not the stallion that initiates the movement of the group – the stallion is more likely to be found trailing behind. In times of danger or alarm, however, the stallion controls the movement of the group, normally by driving them from the rear (see 'Between groups'). The stallion is also the most vigilant member of the group and, especially in the breeding season, he tends to lie down less than the mares.

Friends

Within a group, particular mares tend to associate together; they may be related, but quite often they are not. One of the ways in which they reinforce and maintain this relationship is by grooming each other, usually by nibbling at the other's mane, shoulder, back or rump, first one side then the other – those places that are particularly difficult to reach for oneself. Although a subordinate pony may initiate the grooming, the more dominant one usually ends it, often with a mild ear threat. In summer these mares are commonly found standing together nose to tail swishing flies from each other with their tails. Grooming and fly-swishing benefit both individuals by maintaining the coat in good condition and keeping down the number of flies and other external parasites. Sometimes being too aggressive and dominant can be a disadvantage; for example, 'Light Nose', the most dominant mare in the New Forest group mentioned above, groomed only with the stallion or her foal.

Ponies have individual personalities and needs, but they also like to conform as a group and the chances are that if one pony does something, such as rest, defaecate or go for a drink, others will soon follow suit. This is particularly noticeable between individuals that associate together – and is annoying for the intrepid scientist when all her data arrive at once!

Moods and messages – body language for ponies

A sociable lifestyle in a stable group facilitates the development of communication skills. Ponies can communicate quite complicated messages and emotions using facial expressions, body postures and a variety of noises.

Ear-watching

Always 'watch out for the ears' when you encounter a pony. A pony's highly mobile ears are its most useful communication tool and much can be learned about a pony's emotional state by just watching them; observations of the eyes, mouth and body posture help to complete the picture.

Ears back – fight or flight. Ears laid back along the neck means roughly 'move out of my way or else...' – a threat. They are also laid back when a pony is very frightened and running away from something. When this happens the whites of the eyes show and the nostrils are flared, in order to increase oxygen intake for a fast getaway.

Ears up and forwards – alert, inquisitive and greeting. A pony that has just seen or heard something unusual raises its neck and head, and opens its eyes wide. It may also inflate its nostrils and snort, sometimes repeatedly – making a huffing sort of sound, and raise its tail slightly; there is tension throughout its body which only relaxes if it becomes accustomed to the new stimulus or moves away. This response may develop into a closer investigation of the unknown in which the neck is outstretched and the novelty is inspected with the nose for its feel and smell. When approaching its companions a pony's ears are usually forwards and the eyes wide open, the ponies usually touch noses as they meet, and often make more intimate contact by blowing up each other's nostrils. On many occasions this is followed by a squeal and forekicking of a front hoof. Somewhere between the alert and greeting expression is one which I describe as a 'best face' and is most often seen when food is being offered. The pony looks particularly appealing with its ears forward and eyes wide open, a raised and slightly arched neck with the head held down almost vertical.

Ears up and turned back – alert, listening but... there is something about which it is uncertain happening from behind. This occurs if the pony is startled or if it is pursued from behind. If it moves away it may show the whites of its eyes and clamp its tail down in submission.

'What is it?'

'What does it do?'

'Help!'

'Hello!'

'I'm so hungry.'

'What is that?'

Ears out to the side – the relaxed pony. Resting, sleeping and feeding; the whole body is relaxed.

Noises

Ponies are relatively quiet animals; most of their noises are snorts, coughs and grunts which serve to clear the nasal passages and communicate no more than the fact that they have a fly or some dust up their noses. But they do have a modest repertoire of noises, consisting of a snort, a growl, a squeal, a nicker and a whinny which are all used for specific purposes.

Snorts, sometimes accompanied by a 'huffing' noise, are used by all ponies when alarmed, and by stallions when fighting and when approaching a mare in which they are sexually interested, together with the low, guttural growl. The squeal is used by both sexes when touching noses, during sexual and, to a lesser extent, aggressive encounters.

Nickers and whinnies are the most common noises and are used in a variety of situations, particularly when contact needs to be made. Nickers are relatively low pitched, quiet sounds. They are used for contact and probably reassurance between mares and foals, when approaching group companions, when approaching humans for hand-outs (complete with their 'best face') and also as a mild alarm call to other members of the group in response to the appearance of people or dogs – especially if young foals are being approached. A pony often nickers in response to a whinny by another. The whinny is a louder, higher pitched call which carries further and is mainly used when members of the group or foals and dams have become separated from each other, but may also be used in greeting.

Between groups

Because home ranges of ponies overlap, groups inevitably meet up, especially on prime grazing sites where separate groups graze close to each other. There appears to be an understood minimum allowed distance between groups which, when infringed, may result in an encounter between the stallions. Encounters cost energy and, as with the mares, most stallion-to-stallion encounters are generally display and ritual rather than aggression which might lead to injury; they know where they stand in the stallion hierarchy and so there is no need to waste eating time and energy and risk injury by fighting about it.

This example of a typical meeting between adult New Forest stallions (where both parties know each other) is taken from my own field notes:

'Dun stallion walks towards battle-scarred bay roan, they high-step trot towards each other with arched necks, sniff a dung pile together, throw up their heads and squeal, touch noses and squeal, sniff shoulders and squeal; bay roan stallion kicks out at dun and dungs on existing dung pile, dun adopts dunging posture over another dung pile but does not defaecate; both turn and trot away from each other, the dun shaking his head as he goes.'

In this instance, the bay roan stallion was probably dominant over the dun. Where one or both stallions are newcomers to the area, the confrontation is considerably less peaceable, especially if they are similar in

The art of creating a stud pile.

Herding.

size and experience. The same ritualized high stepping trot and preliminary sniffing occurs but it will be followed by pushing, biting of shoulder, neck, flank and legs, and kicking; in serious fights the stallions will
rear up at each other in order to knock the other off balance. The fight
ends when one stallion either retreats or is chased off by the other.
Injuries can be inflicted during these encounters, especially flesh wounds
and bruising.

A common feature in all stallion encounters is defaecation, or at least
the posture. This behaviour is the stallion's way of marking his presence,
not the result of over-excitement or fear. Dung possesses odours individual to each pony, and in various locations huge piles can be found on
which stallions habitually dung each time they are passing. Some of
these 'stud' piles can become as long as two metres and over half a metre
high! The piles appear to occur randomly within an area so they probably serve just to indicate which stallions have passed that way and when.
Territorial members of the horse family (Grevy's zebra and the asses),
however, use dung to mark their territories and warn other males to
keep out.

After an encounter, a stallion usually gathers his respective mares
together and moves the group further away from the other stallion by
driving them from behind. The herding posture he adopts for this is
unmistakable. He lowers his neck to below the withers, lays his ears half
back and moves his head up and down in a snake-like movement. This
is performed at speeds varying from walk to gallop, but is most often
done in a trot. The mares respond to this gesture by moving ahead of
him, some raising their tails and spurting urine at the same time.

Passing the time

Gorse provides shelter and a good windbreak.

Anybody who has watched ponies for a few hours will have come away with the impression that they spend most of their time eating and standing around doing nothing in particular – and this is not far wrong. The average pony spends about 80% of the day and 60% of the night eating; most of the rest of the time is spent resting, with relatively little time spent in other activities such as moving from one place to another or interacting with other individuals.

The allocation of time to different activities varies with season, time of day and weather, but ponies usually spend most time feeding in the early morning and late afternoon, and take a rest around midday. Over the year, they eat most in spring and in autumn, times when packing in the food is particularly important. In spring this is to make up for shortages of food in the winter and, for mares, to meet the demands of producing a foal (see page 81), and in autumn they need to be able to store away as much fat in their bodies as possible for the approaching winter. They generally spend less time feeding in the summer, especially on hot, sunny days when they pass much of the day standing around nose to tail, swishing flies, often in large groups. In winter, just keeping warm requires a lot of energy. In wet and windy conditions, if sheltered habitats such as woods and gorsebrakes are available, a pony may use less energy by resting in these warmer locations than by feeding in more exposed areas where more energy is spent keeping warm than can be obtained from the food. In areas where there is not much shelter, such as Sable Island, the ponies have to feed almost continuously in the winter, turning their rumps into the wind and clamping their tails firmly down.

On today's menu...

I described earlier how the ability of ponies to eat almost continuously was probably one of the secrets of their success in some areas over the ruminant herbivores (see Food processing). Ponies are also opportunist feeders – that is, they will eat almost any vegetable matter available.

Given the choice, ponies would probably eat grass all year round, and the effects of intensive grazing can be seen in the well trimmed lawns and verges of the New Forest. But grass is not abundant in all areas where ponies live and does not grow all year, so other sources of food have to be found. In temperate areas such as Britain, ponies also eat mosses, sedges, rushes, small amounts of heather and ling, bracken (especially between July and October), leaves of deciduous trees, small forbs such as dandelion and clover, shrubs such as bramble and broom, sweet chestnuts and acorns in autumn, and, from winter to early spring, holly and gorse are probably the most important foods for the survival of some populations.

Holly and gorse may be sharp and prickly but behind this defence they are very nutritious and, where available, form a major part of the diet at a time when little else is in abundance. In the Second World War they were chopped up and added to barley as feed for working horses. How do ponies cope with such a prickly meal? Carefully... They roll back their lips to bite a piece off and carefully manoeuvre it to the back teeth where it is crushed and the prickles rendered harmless. To help them in this, some ponies (both males and females), often deemed to be

Ponies are opportunist feeders.

Careful! Prickly food.

'old types', protect their sensitive upper lips by sporting moustaches in winter, and some have toughened, or 'glazed', tongues. Some ponies also like to soften this prickly food before taking it into the mouth; they bash gorse with a front hoof before eating and with holly they bite a piece off, let it drop to the ground and leave it to wilt for a day or two to soften. Holly and gorse also provide shelter for the pony whilst it is feeding; a gorse bush is an excellent windbreak and a prime place in which to put one's rump in wet and windy weather.

There are many examples of the ability of ponies to make the most of what is available to them. Ponies eat seaweed on the Scottish coast, the Gower peninsula, and the coast of the New Forest. On Assateague

Ponies will dig for food in snow.

The consuming art of topiary – close browsing of holly.

island there is much competition for the highly nutritious, bright green sea lettuce that is thrown onto the beaches by winter storms. Free-ranging horses in southern New Mexico rely on the sugary pods of the mesquite tree for autumn feed and in Brazil the Roraima horse's diet is dominated by cashew fruit. In more harsh climates horses are adept at digging in the snow with their front hooves and muzzles in order to reach food beneath. Some even dig up roots and eat wood, soil and old dung to supplement their diets, which may indicate that they are deficient in minerals such as iron and phosphorous.

... And something to drink

Water is as important to a pony as food, if not more so. If water is short a pony's appetite is reduced and in extreme cases the pony stops eating. The amount of water that a pony drinks each day depends on many factors: the weather, the water content of its food, and the animal itself – its size, whether it is lactating and how active it is, for example. At a rough estimate, a pony living in a temperate climate requires at least 18 litres (4 gallons) of water a day, and during lactation this can increase by up to 70%. Ponies on coastal islands, such as Assateague, which eat a lot of salty food and inevitably drink some salt water, drink about twice as much fresh water as they would need on the mainland in order to flush the excess salt from their bodies. The frequency with which ponies take a drink varies between individuals and populations, and is probably related to the availability and location of the water supply. Groups of ponies go to drink between one and five times a day. A thirsty horse can drink between 3 and 12 litres in a single draught at a rate of 1 litre every 6 seconds!

Horses are resourceful when water is scarce due to drought or frost.

They will dig for water during a drought and will eat snow in winter. Some will travel long distances to reach water; horses in the Pryor Mountains (western US), for example, are known to travel up to ten miles a day. In winter when the water trough was frozen, my own domestic mare had a canny knack of pushing the floating ice of her drinking trough down with her knee in order to drink more easily.

Deviant diets

In the normal course of events, ponies are strict herbivores and do not eat meat. However, meat-eating ponies have existed in both mythology and fact.

In Greek mythology, Diomedes, a tyrannical king of Thrace, fed his mares on the flesh of men who came to visit him. Eurystheus, a cruel and greedy king, wanted these mares, which were reputed to be as fast as the wind, and told Hercules to get them for him as his eighth labour. Diomedes tried to feed Hercules to the mares but in the fight that ensued, Hercules stunned Diomedes and the mares ate their master instead. This meal apparently tamed them and Hercules brought the mares to Eurystheus.

There are a number of real life situations in which horses have been fed meat in order to supplement an inadequate diet: in 1324 during the siege of Metz (Moselle region, north-east France) the horses were fed on meat cut into small pieces and wrapped in bran, and in Mongolia horses going on long journeys are sometimes fed on shrubs and small pieces of dried mutton. In the mountain zones of northern Manchuria (north-east China), horses are actually trained to eat meat; they are first given small bits of salted, dried flesh which are then gradually replaced by raw meat. In Norway, horses and other stock apparently traditionally 'enjoy' boiled fish soup.

The Field *magazine has in the past run articles about carnivorous horses. One article described a horse that was found eating a shelduck 'with apparent enjoyment' and another related the gory tale of a gelding that had developed a liking for savaging ewes – a habit that was attributed to bowel parasites which had given him a craving for meat.*

Other members of the Equidae family are not able to cope with meat so well, and it can be fatal to donkeys, which cannot digest the animal protein. I do not know whether mules suffer the same effects.

Getting up requires energy.

Do ponies sleep standing up?
Yes: in fact they spend more time sleeping standing up than lying down, although most will lie down once a day. If necessary, a horse can remain standing for several days. This is made possible by the 'stay mechanism' of the legs in which the joints are locked into position by a system of muscles and ligaments, in particular the suspensory and check ligaments, which support the muscles and bones of the lower legs, hocks and knees. When sleeping in this position, a pony often rests a hind leg, relaxes its muscles, drops its head to below wither height and closes its eyes; its ears flop out to the side and, in a deep sleep, the lower lip hangs down. Other large herbivores, such as cattle and sheep, do not have a stay mechanism, and spend much more time lying down. Ponies lie down in two ways: on the breastbone with the legs tucked underneath, usually resting the nose on the ground, and laid flat out on their sides with the legs outstretched. Lying down to sleep may appear to us to be more relaxing and to require less energy than standing up, but for a pony this position actually uses more energy because it interferes with breathing and circulation. Ponies also need a good burst of energy in order to heave themselves back onto their feet again. They usually sleep in bouts of 60-90 minutes and when they wake up, like us, they yawn widely and stretch their necks, backs and legs.

In general, foals and yearlings lie down more than adults and, within some free-ranging groups, the stallion rarely lies down.

In hot weather, ponies tend to stand more, which exposes a greater surface area of the pony to the air and allows more heat to be lost. Whilst standing, ponies are also better able to defend themselves against fly attack by stamping, kicking, tail swishing and moving. In cold weather, provided that the ground is dry, lying down with the legs tucked underneath is the better strategy as it reduces exposure to the cold air and so is likely to lessen heat loss. On cold winter nights ponies can be found lying close to each other, presumably to keep warm by sharing the heat from each others' bodies.

Horsing around

Young foals amuse themselves on the shore.

The rest of the pony's time is spent moving from one place to another, usually in search of food or shelter, interacting with other individuals and grooming. Friendly and unfriendly interactions have already been described (see page pp. 49, 51) and in summer many of these interactions have sexual overtones, which will be described later.

Moving about
How far do ponies travel from one place to another? This depends very much on the resources available to them. I have already described how some ponies will walk long distances to find water whilst others, whose resources of food, shelter and water are close at hand, may remain in the same area all day. On the whole, most movement occurs early in the morning and in the evening, often between day- and night-time feeding areas. Whilst feeding, ponies are constantly on the move, albeit very slowly, and they may remain in the same general area all day. Sometimes they will suddenly stop feeding and set off, often at a trot or even canter, to another area. In summer, this sudden movement may be due to excessive aggravation from flies, or another harem grazing too close for comfort, but quite often there is no obvious reason – perhaps they just feel like stretching their legs? Contrary to the popular image of 'wild' horses, free-ranging adult ponies rarely gallop, or even canter, unless they have to, and most only jump if there is no alternative. Especially for mares, conservation of energy is the name of the game.

Foal play

Conserving energy is of little concern to young foals who do not have to look far for a ready supply of high energy food. This allows them to indulge in play, which is an essential part of growing up, and enables the foal to develop its physical and social skills for later life. Most ponies do not initiate play after their first year and most play occurs in the first summer. Older ponies may be drawn into play by foals but their involvement is more tolerance than participation; they rarely have the surplus energy for playing together, unlike their domestic counterparts.

Foals begin to play within their first few days; at this stage their games are either solitary galloping or centred on their mother. She patiently tolerates her mane, tail and legs being chewed, being 'mounted' from all directions and a galloping, bucking, kicking foal which races round her and then uses her in order to stop. Fortunately for the mare, all this calms down after two to three weeks and the foal turns its attentions to other foals of its own age; the play of older, bigger foals is probably too rough. Foals play at chasing and racing, mounting and grooming – which usually starts as friendly nibbling and scratching but which often turns into biting and play aggression and fighting. Fillies and colts play together until the latter are about a month old; after this time the fundamental behaviour differences between the sexes begin to show and the biting, fighting, mounting and chasing games that the colts play are too rough for the fillies who prefer more gentle games of mutual grooming, play aggression and chasing. Some colts and fillies continue to play together but the filly will leave the game if it becomes too rough; if the colt persists, a young filly may even run to her dam – who will show the persistent colt his place! In some cases, however, a colt and filly associate

Colts indulge in mock fights.

and play more with each other than with foals of their own sex. By the time fillies are a year old they play very little, but colts will still play together in their second spring.

Grooming

Grooming maintains the quality of the coat by massaging the skin to improve circulation and by removing dirt and some external parasites (see pp. 93-6). Much grooming is carried out with the help of a friend (see page 51), but ponies also groom themselves by rubbing on trees and posts, nibbling themselves and rolling. These activities are particularly frequent in spring and early summer when ponies are changing coats. Rolling also helps to dry a pony off after rain or a swim.

What goes in must come out ...

Dung for scientists.

Dung ... the mainstay of roses and rhubarb. Owing to their 'bulk is best' feeding strategy, ponies produce vast quantities of the stuff – deemed by one eminent biologist to be 'the bread and butter of ecology'. Although I may not go quite that far, it certainly is useful, not only to the scientist but also to the animals themselves.

Dung is the portion of an animal's food which has passed undigested through the gut, stuck together with a good helping of mucus. For a pony this amounts to a good proportion of its coarse, fibrous intake. Most food reappears as dung about two days after it was ingested, although very fibrous material may take up to four days to complete its journey. Ponies defaecate many times during the day and, having had the dubious privilege of spending many hours waiting for 'samples', I have found that this usually occurs every two or three hours. The quantity produced depends upon the quantity and digestibility of the food the pony has eaten.

From a dung pile you can tell what the pony has been eating (and therefore some idea as to where it has been), the kind of internal parasites it has and, if you are another pony, its sex, reproductive state and probably which individual it is. A word of caution; most of the areas in Britain where ponies are free-ranging are SSSIs, National Parks, or otherwise protected areas, so remember that it is illegal to take dung, for whatever purpose (once it has hit the ground ...) without permission.

'Hmm ... one of mine.'

What's he dung?

I described earlier how a stallion usually defaecates at the end of an encounter with another stallion and on the 'stud' piles in order to mark his presence (see page 56). Throughout the day, especially during the breeding season, a stallion regularly inspects and smells dung piles in his area and those that he comes across when moving from place to place. He either 'marks' the pile by defaecating or urinating on it or 'rejects' it and moves on. Fresh dung piles attract the most attention; piles which are a day or more old are either not inspected or are rejected. Having labelled numerous New Forest dung piles according to their mare of origin and then noted the stallion's response to them, I found that those the stallion marked came from mature mares usually found in his group, and those he rejected belonged to immature mares in the group or mares not seen with the group. Why does he do this? The stallion is probably able to identify the dung of individual mares; consequently he can put his own smell onto the dung of those most valuable to him, which will indicate to another stallion his presence, that the mare belongs to him and probably also cover up the smell of a mare that is in season.

Mares will also sniff the dung of other mares and stallions, but they do not do this as frequently as the stallions and only occasionally do they dung, urinate or exhibit flehmen over the pile. On the other hand, foals frequently investigate their mother's dung; they usually paw it first, eat some and then urinate on it.

Dung also acts as a feeding deterrent. Unless food is very scarce, horses will not feed close to their own dung. This is the case with many her-

'I'll make sure the others know it.'

bivores, such as cattle, but horses go one step further and designate whole areas as 'latrines' in which they defaecate and urinate but do not feed. This is particularly obvious in a field grazed only by horses where about a third of the area is ungrazed and consequently consists of long grass and more weeds like thistles and buttercup than the rest of the field. This may seem like a waste of good grazing area, but there is a very sound reason for it. By confining defaecation and urination to a part of the field which is not grazed, the risk of infection by bacteria, parasite eggs and other pathogens passed out in the urine and faeces is reduced. One way of overcoming this waste is to graze cattle or sheep with horses; cattle and sheep will feed in the horses' latrine area, and horses will feed close to the cattle and sheep dung. For each species, ingestion of most of the parasites and pathogens passed out by the other is unlikely to cause much harm and, in the case of parasites, passage through the gut of the wrong host renders them harmless.

There are exceptions to every rule and on occasion ponies will eat dung. As noted above, this is particularly common for foals, which eat their mother's dung – a practice which is believed to help the foal acquire the correct gut flora to cope with its free-ranging life. In the western USA, horses have been recorded eating dung during exceptionally severe conditions; but only dung that was old, and presumbly less harmful, was taken.

Dung for scientists

How can dung tell us what the pony has eaten? Although some signs of food items are obvious to the naked eye, such as acorn or chestnut husks, a microscope is needed to identify most plants. This is made possible by the fact that each species of plant has a unique cell wall shape and tissue pattern which, for most species, remain intact during passage through the gut. Some of these are really quite attractive; bracken, for example, looks like a very complicated jigsaw puzzle, and the cell walls of Agrostis curtisii (bristle agrostis) and Molinia cerulea (purple moor grass) look like unravelled knitting wool. Although some plants are more easily recognized than others and some are more digestible and therefore more difficult to see, this technique does provide a good estimation of a pony's diet.

Microscopic analysis is also used to identify the eggs of internal parasites passed out in the dung. Like all 'wild' animals ponies carry their fair share of internal parasites, or 'worms', in the gut – amongst other places (see pp. 97–9). These parasites lay eggs which are passed out of the pony in the dung. The eggs are frequently very difficult to identify to the species of parasite, even with a microscope, and often have to be incubated until they become larvae. Some idea of the type of internal parasites carried by a pony can be gained from the dung, although this technique is not reliable for estimating the numbers of parasites carried by a pony, as the eggs are not released into the gut at a constant rate. More will be said of these internal lodgers later on.

A new generation

In order to sustain their populations, ponies must produce sufficient offspring to replace the adults that die. In many populations mares produce a foal every year but in harsh environments, such as on Sable Island, many of the foals die in their first year. In most of the British populations, mares usually foal in two out of every three years or every other year, but most foals survive. Successful reproduction requires the ponies to have reached sexual maturity and to be in sufficiently good body condition to conceive, to carry the foal full term and finally to feed it during its early months. These requirements are better met at some times of the year than at others.

Puberty
The onset of puberty in horses depends not only on age but also on growth rate and nutrition. In domestic horses, well nourished fillies and colts can reach puberty at about one year of age; but free-ranging ponies, which live on a poorer diet and grow more slowly, rarely reach puberty until they are at least two. Colts are usually able to sire foals when they are two (although few get the opportunity until they are older) but most mares do not produce a foal until they are four or five. Mares can continue producing foals for many years, and there are many great-great grandmothers still giving birth at over twenty years of age. Stallions are capable of breeding throughout their lives but in unmanaged populations, many do not breed when they are young or very old because they cannot maintain a harem.

Sexy signals
A mare uses some very clear signals to let a stallion know whether or not she is receptive to his advances. She is most receptive when in oestrous ('season' or 'heat'). This is the time when ova are released and if the mare is covered by a stallion she is likely to conceive. When not in oestrous, attention from a stallion, usually in the form of sniffing the mare's shoulder or tail region, is met either with total indifference or, more often, aggression. When the mare is in oestrous it is a different story. If a stallion is nearby and approaches, or in some cases just looks at her, she adopts a posture in which she stands with her back legs apart and her tail raised, usually urinating a little and 'winking' by protruding

71

'She's far too young.'

her clitoris through her vulval lips (entrance to the vagina). If the stallion was not already paying her attention, he usually gets the message from this seductive pose! Some mares will actually present themselves to the stallion, others wait for him to make the first move.

There are some instances when this oestrous posture is not sufficiently enticing for a stallion. This is the sad case for many love-lorn two to three-year-old fillies which, from their behaviour, appear to be in oestrous for a long time, sometimes up to thirty days. Despite constantly flaunting themselves by adopting the oestrous posture and remaining as close to the stallion as he will allow, they are at best ignored by him or, more often, chased away (but their ardour is constant and they are soon back to try again!). Why should a male reject a female which is apparently showing all the signs that she is receptive and fertile? It is probably because these fillies do not smell right. The advances that a stallion makes to a mare always involve some preliminary sniffing around the top of the tail and often the urine itself. The odours of the urine and vaginal secretions are likely to provide the stallion with the true picture of the mare's reproductive state and, despite the exaggerated oestrous behaviour of these fillies, the stallion can smell that they are not worth the effort of covering. The fertility of these fillies is believed to be low and, if they do conceive, abortion is common.

The clinch
If the mare smells right then the stallion will begin courting in earnest.

'Smells good to me.'

Some stallions are clearly more 'gentlemanly' about this process than others (and, to be fair, some mares are more ladylike than others). Sometimes a stallion will approach a mare apparently without any obvious provocation or sign from her, but more often the wooing is initiated by the mare urinating; she may move closer to the stallion to do this. The stallion will smell the urine, and from my own observations it seems that he actually draws some up into his nostrils; he then almost invariably raises his head and exhibits flehmen (see Special equipment). Whilst emitting a low, growling sound, he then moves over to the mare in question, who is probably standing in the oestrous posture, and begins a series of sniffs and nuzzles, which are presumably designed to persuade the mare to succumb to his charms (some mares need more persuading than others). The couple usually begin by touching noses and blowing up each other's nostrils; then the stallion starts sniffing and sometimes nibbling along the mare's neck, up and down her shoulder, flank, and then to her tail and vulval region. Some stallions spend more time on

No privacy.

these preliminaries than others. This is all accompanied by a variety of squeals from both individuals, more growling from the stallion, and some kicking with the foreleg, particularly by the mare. If things go to plan and the mare stands still, the stallion is able to mount and copulate successfully. However, this is not always the case and often at the tail and vulval sniffing stage the mare tries to move away or kick out at the stallion with her hind legs. In response, the more gentlemanly stallion usually returns to sniffing and nibbling of the shoulder or moves away, but the rougher, often younger, male is more impatient and will attempt to mount and copulate, even though the mare is moving. If the mare continues to move, the stallion finds it difficult to keep up with her on only two legs and usually ends up losing his grip and dismounting before ejaculation. With a little more patience, the mare is usually persuaded to stand whilst mounted and copulation is successful. After copulation, which lasts just a few seconds, the mare usually stands in the oestrous posture, often dribbling urine, whilst the stallion will sometimes smell the ground and exhibit flehmen.

Privacy during these intimate moments is something that ponies do not have. Throughout the process, other members of the group, especially the young, gather round and watch.

A stallion will usually copulate with a mare a number of times whilst she is in oestrous, especially if she is a member of his group, and during this time she tends to feed and rest close to him. In some managed populations where mares are not always in a permanent group with a stallion (see An unnatural group), apparently chance encounters with oestrous mares occur. Sometimes this is purely by chance and at other times it seems that the receptive, oestrous mare is out looking for a stallion. Some mares can be quite fickle. I remember one mare who left the stallion she had been ranging with for another about fifty metres away; she copulated with the latter and then calmly returned to the former. The stallion chosen by the mare was older and had been resident in the area for longer than the other. There was no confrontation between the two stallions, but both herded their respective mares away.

A time to breed

Most ponies have a specific breeding season during which conception, the final stages of pregnancy and birth takes place. In temperate climates this is from spring to autumn. Suckling a foal demands much energy from a mare especially in the first three months, and so it makes sense to produce a foal when the weather is relatively mild and food is abundant and nutritious. During this time mares which are not pregnant come into oestrous about every 3 weeks, usually for 4-6 days. Once conception has taken place, no more ova are released until after the birth or the mare aborts. Outside the breeding season, mares are 'anoestrous', that is they do not produce ova.

The timing of this breeding season is probably controlled by day length, although other factors such as weather and availability of food and water are inevitably closely linked with day length and may be equally important. In different parts of the world which experience different day lengths the breeding season varies accordingly. Ponies living in areas at higher latitudes where summers are shorter have correspondingly short breeding seasons, while ponies in tropical regions, where the sun is overhead twice a year and days are always at least ten hours long, often have two breeding seasons.

A breeding season may be a feature of the more primitive and relatively 'unimproved' breeds, especially ponies. 'Improved' breeds like the Thoroughbreds are able to breed all year. The 'official birthday' of all Thoroughbreds is January 1st – hardly a good time of the year for a pony fending for itself in the northern hemisphere to produce a foal, but in the controlled environment of a stud farm this is not a problem. There are some free-ranging populations in which mares come into oestrous throughout the year, such as mares in central Australia, Nevada and Sable Island, although in reality most Nevada and Sable Island mares conceive and foal between spring and autumn when the foals are most likely to survive and the mares are in good enough condition to conceive. All of these populations are descendants of 'improved', domestic stock, so they may not be able to respond to environmental factors in the same way as the 'less improved' populations.

Pregnancy

Pregnancy normally lasts for about eleven months but its length can be affected by a number of factors. Colt foals take from two to seven days longer than fillies. Pregnancy may be longer if the foal was conceived, and so is due, early in the year, and if the mare is poorly nourished or in poor condition; it may be shorter if the mare conceived later in the year. This all helps to ensure that foals are born at the time of the year when environmental conditions are most favourable for their growth and for the mare to meet the energy requirements of lactation.

Being pregnant has very little effect on the mare until the last four months when the foal begins to grow most rapidly, especially during the final month. During this time the mare's energy requirements increase by 5-20%. Until the last 2-6 weeks of pregnancy, the mare's udder with its two teats is usually quite small and inconspicuous, unless she has had a lot of foals, but during these final weeks it fills out and 'drops' – the mare is 'bagged up'. In the few days before giving birth the teats fill out and a waxy substance from the colostrum forms on their tips.

Abortion

Abortion is known to occur in both the early and late stages of pregnancy, but few aborted foetuses are ever found because of the efficiency of scavengers such as foxes, crows and buzzards, and so data on this are scant. Abortion may be due to a number of factors such as sickness of the mare, bacterial infection and malformation or death of the foetus. For ponies, however, probably the most common cause is malnutrition and poor body condition of the mare. If a mare is in poor condition before foaling she is unlikely to have sufficient energy reserves to produce enough milk to rear the foal. Abortion of the foal at least gives her a chance of making up condition and improving the likelihood of her conceiving in the next season.

It's a foal!

Most foals are born at night or very early in the morning. In the few hours before the event the mare becomes increasingly restless and sweats profusely. In some populations it is common for a mare to leave her group at this time but, whether alone or with the group, she will usually select a birth site with complete ground cover and, if available, some overhead cover too. Birth itself is usually very quick; after the waters have broken (releasing between 9 and 23 litres of fluid) it can take only five minutes, and the whole process normally takes less than an hour. If the mare is disturbed, she can prolong the preliminary stages before the waters break. Most mares give birth lying down and remain so for about half an hour after the foal has been born. Giving birth is an exhausting process, even if it does not take very long. The foal should arrive head first, with its forelegs extended and its head and neck resting on them. The majority of mares give birth without obvious difficulty but, because so few births of free-ranging foals are seen, the frequency of breach and other abnormal births is not known. The afterbirth is usually passed out by the mare ten to fifteen minutes after the foal has been born, although it can take up to two hours; she does not eat the placenta, but it is soon cleared up by local scavengers. The size of the foal at birth is primarily controlled by the size of the mare – small mare, small foal. The production of twins is very rare in free-ranging populations.

After birth, the mare usually ignores the foal until it starts to move; she is probably too exhausted to be bothered with it before this time. Almost immediately after birth the newborn foal breaks out of the foetal membranes, usually using a foreleg and its muzzle. After a short rest, it crawls forward on its front legs towards the mare's head, where the mare sniffs and licks it all over. Licking dries the foal's coat and it is also thought to help establish the bond between mare and foal. The umbilical cord is broken when either the mare or foal stands up. The foal often has to make a number of attempts in order to stand, and its first few steps are invariably wobbly and lacking in co-ordination. If the mare is standing and the foal is not she will normally encourage it to get up by nudging it with her muzzle. Most foals make it onto their hooves within an hour. Once both are up they move away from the birth site, where the placenta and birth fluids may attract predators. If there is a problem with the foal, such as malformation of the limbs or stillbirth, the mare continues to try and get it to stand up, but if there is no response after a few hours she will eventually give up and abandon it.

Early days

The foal is normally able to find the udder without difficulty. If it does not, the mare helps by pushing it in the right direction. Prior to suckling, many newborn foals push their heads against the udder for several seconds – a practice which probably stimulates the flow of milk. The first udderfuls of milk that the foal drinks provide it with colostrum which contains antibodies to protect the foal from infection and which is vital to its survival. Colostrum also acts as a laxative. Most mares make suckling a little easier for the new foal by standing still and making the teats more accessible by flexing the hind leg furthest from the foal. The mare ends these early suckling bouts by moving, and by doing so she encourages the hungry foal to follow her and no other mare or moving object.

Young mares foaling for the first time will sometimes reject their foals, and this occasionally happens with older animals. These mares may be particularly sensitive around the teats and move away every time the foal attempts to suckle. The foal usually persists for two to three hours and, if still unsuccessful, it moves away and attempts to suckle anything. Other mares will almost invariably reject the foal, although it may just be lucky enough to find a mare whose foal has died and which may allow it to suckle – but this is rare. As time goes on, if its dam continues to reject it, the foal weakens and its drive to suckle decreases. If the weather is cold and wet it may take as little as six hours for the foal to become too weak to hold its head up to suckle; eventually it will die.

Sometimes a mare will accept an orphan foal if it does not smell of another mare.

'Lovely!'

In the normal course of events a mare is very protective of her new-born foal, which is often a source of much interest to other members of the group. She becomes aggressive to other group members (which may result in a temporary rise in her position in the dominance hierarchy) and keeps the foal near to her and away from the other ponies who might harm or steal it.

Dominant mares whose foals were stillborn have been known to steal a subordinate mare's foal. In general, though, persuading a mare to foster the foal of another is very difficult unless the foal does not smell of another pony. In the domestic situation this can be achieved by dowsing the foal in substances such as talcum powder, linseed oil or even whisky, but this is rarely possible in a free-ranging situation.

Mares come into season again one to twelve days after giving birth; this is known as 'foal heat' or 'post-partum oestrous'. Fertility is believed to be good at this time. In the deserts of North America and on Assateague about 80% of mares conceive if covered at this time, but in the New Forest the figure is about 20%. If the mare does not conceive whilst in foal heat her normal three-week oestrous cycle resumes.

The milk bar

For foals

Milk is essential for the healthy growth and development of the foal. Foals deprived of milk during their first three to four months rarely grow as well as those that received a good supply at this time, and there is evidence to suggest that foals that suckled through their first winter will maintain better body condition in the future.

As with all new mothers, a mare's life is considerably disrupted and disturbed by the demands of her new offspring. In its first week, a foal suckles for about 80 seconds an average of four times every hour of the day and night. As it grows older and grazes more it suckles less; at one month of age it suckles for about a minute three times an hour, by two months this has declined to about one minute per hour and by eight months it is down to once every two hours – which usually continues until weaning (see below). Suckling is frequently preceded by a 'permission to feed' movement, in which the foal goes to the front of the mare, sometimes under her neck, before moving to the udder. This behaviour is often accompanied by a toss of the head and a nicker (see page 54), and may be repeated if the mare does not allow the foal to feed. The foal usually suckles with its body alongside its mother and its rear end near her head – for some very young foals this position also provides some extra stability! If it becomes too rough in its suckling, the foal is also in a very good position to receive a timely bite on the rump or hind legs; most foals disregard this and either kick out at the mare or move their body away from her side.

Suckling bouts take place most commonly after the foal has been resting, when either the mare or the foal approaches the other or after a

period of separation. In some populations, they coincide with the mares' main feeding times of morning and evening; but in areas like the Camargue where fly attack is a major problem to the horses, the foals tend to suckle more in the daytime when the mares are standing still, shading, rather than at night when they are more active and feeding.

During their first eight weeks, colt foals appear to be far more greedy than fillies. Some spend up to 40% more time suckling, although mares suckling colts do not necessarily lose more body condition than those suckling fillies. Colts are also not necessarily heavier than fillies of the same age, and the longer time spent suckling may be due to greater energy demands caused by their more energetic play (see page 65). On the other hand, perhaps colts are just slower sucklers than fillies.

For mares
Suckling a foal has a major effect on the physiology of the mare. In the first three months of lactation her daily energy requirements can increase by up to 70%. It is not surprising that during this period mares increase the time that they spend feeding and some may change their habitat use and diet to increase their energy intake. Some mares suffer much loss of body condition during the early months of lactation, especially those that foal early in the season when their body fat reserves are depleted and food is less plentiful.

To wean or not to wean ...
Foals begin to nibble grass from the day that they are born; they also nibble all sorts of other things including rocks, wood, soil and shrub and tree leaves. This is more exploration than feeding and they do not begin to eat grass until they are three to four days old. Grass consumption increases markedly at around six days when their first incisor teeth come through. Like most young mammals, foals copy what their mothers do, and eat. I have seen foals nibbling gorse when only a few weeks old and readily eating holly in their first winter.

In the managed British populations most foals are removed from their dams in the autumn when aged about four months. Once the dam has overcome the loss of her foal, usually after a day or so if the foal is out of earshot, its removal enables her to improve her body condition (see page 84) and her chances of foaling the following summer.

If the foal is not removed and the dam is not pregnant, she may continue to suckle it well into its second, and sometimes its third year although the amount of milk that the young pony takes by then is small.

If the dam is pregnant, in most populations she will wean the foal a few weeks before the birth of the next. An exception to this is found on Sable Island where mares may continue to suckle the previous year's foal right up to the birth of the next, and some mares will even suckle both together. Even if the yearling has been weaned, should the new foal die, these mares will allow the yearling to resume suckling. It seems odd that in a location where conditions are very harsh, the mares will invest so much energy in lactation. One possible explanation for this is that, if suckling for longer improves a pony's ability to maintain good condition in later life, this may be a sound investment on an island where you need to be very fit to survive. Alternatively, since about 50% of foals born on Sable Island die in their first year, it makes sense to invest heavily in those that survive. This has not been reported from other harsh environments, except for a single case on Assateague where a two-year-old resumed suckling after a foal had been removed in the autumn. The filly continued to suckle until she was nearly three, when the mare died – possibly because of the stress of producing so much milk.

Health and welfare

Most ponies are remarkably healthy throughout their lives, considering the hazards they face whilst fending for themselves and the relatively harsh conditions in which some live. Since few ponies are observed on a regular basis, many ailments must come and go undetected. Ponies experience problems associated with food, disease and parasites, and on a day-to-day basis they receive their fair share of knocks and cuts – especially young stallions who face aggression from both mares and other stallions. Like most wild animals, free-ranging ponies also undergo natural cycles of fatness and leanness governed by food availability and seasonal conditions.

Natural cycles
It is often claimed that ponies in Britain are poor, thin and 'starving to death', especially in spring. Whilst it is true that some animals become excessively thin and have to be taken off the Forest or moor, a loss of body condition (defined here as the amount of fat laid down in the body) at certain times of the year is perfectly natural. Ponies have an annual cycle of body condition; that is to say that the amount of fat that they have stored in the body changes over the year, according to supply and demand. Most other wild herbivores have a similar cycle of condition, which the casual observer does not notice. Ponies are very much under the public eye, which is used to seeing domestic horses and ponies maintained in prime condition for working; these horses and ponies are protected from the seasonal changes in weather and food supply that affect their free-ranging relatives.

As fat is used up the appearance of the pony changes.

Apparently 'poor' ponies can be remarkably fast and agile.

Body condition is best (ponies are fattest) in late summer and early autumn, and poorest (ponies are most lean) in late winter and spring. Condition is directly related to the difference between the energy that ponies are able to take in through their food supply, and the amount that they have to expend on basic functions such as growth, reproduction and maintaining a stable body temperature. During the summer, ponies take in more energy than they need, unless they are lactating, and store the surplus in the body as fat, which is laid down under the skin, in the abdomen, around the organs and in the bone marrow. During the winter and early spring, when there may not be enough energy available from food to meet their needs, they turn to their reserve supply of fat. If ponies are unable to take in enough energy in summer, whether because of insufficient suitable food, problems in processing food due to teeth (see page 35), infection or worms (see pp. 90-91, 97-9), they will not have an adequate reserve for the rigours of winter.

As fat is used up, the external appearance of the pony changes noticeably as the ribs, spine and pelvis begin to show under the skin. A thin pony is not necessarily unwell and I have seen many thin, alert ponies with bright eyes and shiny coats. Problems arise once all the body fat has been used up when, if the energy supply does not improve, muscle protein is broken down to produce energy as a last resort. This causes the pony to weaken quickly and, if more energy does not become available, it will die. A pony which has used up its fat reserves in early or mid-winter is in a far worse situation than one whose reserves last until spring or early summer when new, nutritious growth is soon to become available.

In unmanaged populations ponies die from starvation or disease brought on by malnutrition when winter conditions are particularly harsh, especially following a dry summer when there was insufficient food to build up fat reserves. In this way, the weaker members of the population are removed, leaving those most able to cope with poor environmental conditions to survive to breed the following year.

Whilst this loss is accepted in 'wild', unmanaged populations, for British managed ponies it is not. Although in remote areas (such as certain parts of the Welsh hills, Dartmoor, Exmoor and the New Forest) a few deaths inevitably occur from starvation, measures are taken to prevent this. Ponies found to be in poor condition, especially during early winter, are removed from their free-ranging area to alternative accommodation. This is usually a field where they can be fed hay, or in some cases silage, to supplement grazing. Some ponies are easier to catch and confine than others – apparently 'poor' ponies can be remarkably fast and agile. One February, the capture of a New Forest mare seen to be in poor condition had to be abandoned in order to save a fence after she, her foal and yearling had galloped over it four times (they were all eventually caught quietly a few days later)! The condition of most ponies improves in captivity, given supplies of correct and sufficient food, although the level of stress that individuals suffer in confinement differs widely. Some refuse to eat and pace the perimeter of the field looking for a way out. If they do not escape but continue to refuse to eat, there is no alternative but to return them to the Forest or moor if they are to have a chance of survival.

Beginning to end

Some ponies live on into their twenties, or, occasionally, like an Exmoor stallion I knew, into their thirties; in general, they live shorter lives than their domestic counterparts. Stallions generally live a few years longer than mares, presumably because they do not undergo the physical stress of producing and rearing a foal most years. Many ponies of unmanaged populations die within their first year; on Sable Island up to 50% die, most within their first few days, usually because the mare cannot or will not suckle them. In managed populations, foal mortality is lower, but many owners cull old ponies which cannot maintain condition without assistance.

Old, badly injured or very sick ponies usually leave their group and many wander away to die in an area out of their normal home range. Live ponies show little interest in their dead companions, except for young foals whose mothers have died.

Digestive difficulties

Grass clippings are an attractive meal for ponies – but can cause colic.

We have seen that food shortages can cause problems, but abundance of certain foods can also lead to serious illness.

Colic

This is a collective term used for most equine digestive disorders. Ponies cannot vomit (the nature of the muscles of the lower oesophagus prevents this), so they can experience major problems if they eat something that disagrees with them. What goes down cannot come back up and if the stomach becomes highly distended, it is likely to rupture. Colic in domestic horses is relatively easy to treat but, because most free-ranging ponies can neither be found nor handled easily, it can cause them much distress and in some cases can be fatal – especially if the pony rolls. Rolling is a common response to the discomfort caused by colic, but with colic it can result in the pony either twisting its gut, thereby causing a permanent blockage, or ending up stuck upside down ('cast') in a ditch.

Ponies get colic for a variety of reasons; internal parasites are a common cause (see pp. 97-9) but another, preventable, cause is the consumption of grass clippings. Where ponies live near residential areas, misguided people put grass clippings out for them to eat – which they do with relish. Within a very short time this appetizing pile of fresh green grass begins to ferment and, if eaten, causes colic. In popular tourist areas ponies can suffer from eating meat pies, crisps, biscuits, sandwiches, and anything else that can be scrounged or stolen from the picnic or tent.

However, relatively few cases of colic are reported in the prime scrounging areas of the New Forest and Dartmoor and on the beaches of Assateague – which says something for the constitution of these ponies!

Food poisoning
In its search for food, the opportunist pony will sometimes eat something that contains toxins. Although such foods may not be fatal at the time, after a number of years the damage that they cause to the liver (whose job it is to break the toxins down) can eventually become too great, and the pony will suddenly and rapidly lose condition. This is particularly common for ponies over fifteen years old; post mortem examination of these animals will often reveal a discoloured, badly damaged liver. Ponies rarely eat plants like ragwort, yew and deadly nightshade, which contain compounds that are immediately and fatally toxic, but there are other foods containing toxins which at certain times of the year form a substantial part of a pony's diet in some areas. Bracken and acorns are two important examples.

Bracken – nice and green, but ... bracken *(Pteridium aquilinum)* contains thiaminase, the enzyme that breaks down Vitamin B1 (thiamine). Ponies that eat bracken can therefore become deficient in Vitamin B1. Bracken may also be carcinogenic; it contains ptequiloside, a chemical

Bracken: nice and green, but ...

which is known to cause cancer in cattle. Ponies eat most bracken between July and September when it is mature and the most poisonous, young stage is over, but cases of poisoning still occur. Ponies with bracken poisoning (often called 'staggers') lack co-ordination – symptoms which can easily be confused with an injury to the back or neck. If these symptoms are detected quickly the pony can usually be saved by injections of Vitamin B1 given over a few days. Bracken is not a particularly preferred food and nutritionally it is virtually worthless; it is usually eaten simply because it is there. In times of drought, however, it is one of the few sources of green food, and its consumption increases accordingly, as do the number of cases of poisoning.

Acorns – 'When they're good, they're very, very good, but when they're bad ...' Acorns provide an excellent source of fat and protein – just what a pony needs in the autumn to build up its fat reserves for the winter. There is no doubt that ponies love them and will spend many hours sifting through the leaf litter in an oak wood. Individuals that eat acorns are usually in better condition than those living in the same area that do not; unless, that is, the acorns kill them ...

The reasons why acorns kill ponies are not fully understood. Some die because their guts are blocked by the indigestible husks; this might explain why pigs, which shell acorns before eating them, suffer no ill effects. If the pony is found in time (and is sufficiently amenable), this can be relieved by administering copious quantities of Epsom salts, liquid paraffin and similar laxatives and lubricants. Most deaths due to acorns probably involve some kind of cumulative poisoning, although little is known about the source and identity of the toxin or toxins involved. Cattle are thought to be poisoned by an excess of oak tannins but this is not necessarily the case for ponies. A pony with acute poisoning suffers the sudden onset of diarrhoea and scouring, and the bowel becomes enlarged. These symptoms may be caused by an allergic reaction to the high protein level in the acorns and the pony can sometimes be saved by a vet. Chronic poisoning is common and by the time the symptoms appear, aptly described as 'sleepy staggers', it is too late to do anything. Post mortem examination of these ponies usually reveals that the liver has degenerated into a pulp.

Many ponies eat acorns for years and maintain good condition but suddenly die, often after eating just a few. Tolerance to toxins probably varies from pony to pony, and there are no clear correlations between poisoning and age and sex. It has also been suggested that the chemical composition of the acorns themselves varies from year to year and area to area. It is believed that there is something addictive in acorns – which might explain this apparent craving for something that can be fatal.

In the New Forest, where about 18% of the total area available to the ponies is mature oak and beech woodland, pigs are allowed out onto the Forest for a few weeks in the autumn (the 'pannage' season) in order to reduce the quantity of acorns available to ponies and cattle.

'Something addictive in acorns.'

Disease

Ponies are subject to many minor infections and ailments, most of which go unnoticed. A pony's ability to resist infection is usually related to age and body condition; the very young and old and those in poor condition are most vulnerable. Young ponies have less acquired immunity, and old and poor ponies have fewer reserves of energy with which to fight infection. Serious infections may be part of the pony's general environment or they may be brought into the area from outside by contact with other animals. The most common ones of temperate climates are described below.

Strangles

This is a bacterial infection of *Streptococcus equi* which appears in populations from time to time and is passed between individuals by water droplets, for example through coughs and sneezes. It is an aptly named disease in which the upper respiratory tract becomes inflamed and pus-filled abscesses form on the lymph nodes between the chin and the bottom of the neck, making eating, drinking and, in some cases, breathing uncomfortable and difficult. In particularly bad cases abscesses also form on the body surface or internal organs; this is known as 'bastard strangles'. The abscesses last for up to about ten days, but when they eventually burst the strangled pony feels relief immediately.

Prevention and treatment are difficult, even if the pony can be handled, although some people believe that giving antibiotics in the final stages reduces the risk of pulmonary infection should a burst abscess drain into the lungs. The disease occurs most frequently in young ponies, but once they have had it they are immune. Consequently it appears in waves in populations when there is a sufficient number of ponies which have not yet been infected. It is rarely fatal, although secondary infections can cause problems.

Equine influenza

This is a viral infection, the symptoms of which are similar to those of human 'flu. Although the 'flu itself is rarely fatal, ponies are particularly susceptible to secondary infections such as pneumonia. The virus is droplet borne and so spreads rapidly within a population. In 1989 there was a major outbreak in Britain which spread quickly amongst free-ranging ponies and unvaccinated domestic horses and ponies. Ponies in the New Forest and on Dartmoor were particularly affected. The symptoms began with a bad cough and were followed by a streaming nose; the lungs of the ponies that died were horribly congested. In the New Forest the first cases were reported in late July, with the final cases in September. It arrived on Dartmoor about a month later. Over fifty ponies died in the New Forest, most of a pneumonia secondary to the 'flu. Reliable statistics are not available for Dartmoor. Deaths were not related to the ponies' ages or body conditions, and in the New Forest many good, young ponies were lost. Even if ponies were found with the disease and could be handled, nothing could be done to help them once the symptoms had appeared – they either recovered through their own resistance and strength or they did not. On Exmoor, no cases were reported in the free-ranging Exmoor ponies (although I did observe coughing and a runny nose in a couple of cross-bred ponies on the moor), even though outbreaks occurred in domestic horses in the area. Perhaps, owing to the relatively low numbers of ponies on Exmoor, there was not enough contact between domestic and free-ranging individuals for the infection to spread, or maybe the Exmoors were for some reason immune to the infection.

During this epidemic, the movement of all horses and ponies in England was virtually stopped; shows, hunts and events were cancelled, and in the New Forest and some parts of Dartmoor the annual rounding up of the ponies was either postponed or cancelled. Although it is possible to vaccinate against equine 'flu, this is not practicable for most free-ranging ponies; not only is it expensive but it also involves three injections in the first year followed by annual boosters – and most ponies cannot be caught up to order. One consolation for the 1989 outbreak is that ponies that survived probably now possess some immunity to similar infections in the future.

Tetanus ('lockjaw')

This is an infection by the bacterium *Clostridium tetani* which enters the body through an open wound. Ponies are particularly susceptible to tetanus because the bacteria are present in the soil and their dung. The infection affects the nervous system and causes the muscles to become rigid or go into spasm. It is nearly always fatal, and death is usually by asphyxiation, brought about by the rigidity of the muscles of respiration. Even if it is detected early, treatment is usually ineffectual and by the time the symptoms of general stiffness and a locked jaw occur it is

usually too late. A vaccine for tetanus is available but, like the 'flu vaccine, it is expensive and involves two injections in the first year followed by an annual booster. Ponies on the southern (Virginia) half of Assateague are vaccinated but most ponies elsewhere are not.

Equine infectious anaemia

This is a viral infection which does not occur in Britain but is common in North America, Europe and Asia. It is also known as swamp fever, pernicious equine anaemia and horse malaria. It is transmitted in blood and other body fluids by flies and mosquitoes and most commonly occurs in low-lying, swampy areas. The disease can be fatal and infected ponies are generally unthrifty and weak. Some appear to recover but they still carry the virus and are able to infect others (via flies and mosquitoes), and they may suffer a relapse later on, especially if stressed.

Sea ponies

Assateague ponies take to the sea in order to seek refuge from flies. They sometimes wade out as much as half a mile from the shore and also venture out into the waves for short periods, leaving the smaller foals on the shore; some take a bath as the waves break over them, which cools them and removes the flies.

Ponies living on the Llanrhidian saltmarsh in the north of the Gower peninsula also go into the sea, but not necessarily to avoid the flies. At high tide, some ponies find themselves cut off from dry land by a wall, and they have no choice but to get wet. But this predicament does not seem to be a problem to these ponies that appear to understand the nature of the tides in the area, how they vary and where the water will be each day. They are able to select the best place in which to stand and mares with foals select a spot where the water will not come in above the heads of their foals.

Lodgers and visitors

All animals, including humans, have parasites lodging and visiting outside and inside the body. When low in number, parasites usually have little effect on the well-being of their hosts, but a high population can cause many health problems. Ponies carry a variety of external and internal parasites, the quantity and nature of which depend on where the pony lives, its body condition and its management. I shall describe the parasites of temperate populations here, in particular the British ones. Ponies living elsewhere, especially in hot climates, suffer different forms of infestation.

Lice and ticks

In the late winter, ponies can become infested with the biting and bloodsucking lice *Damalina equi* and *Haematopinus asini*. These are tiny arthropods which are responsible for much irritation and subsequent loss of hair at a time when a pony can least afford a hole in its coat. They cause severe itching, which can result in the pony rubbing itself raw, and heavy infestations can cause anaemia. Both species spend their entire lives from egg to adult (about two months) clinging to the hairs of a pony's coat. They need a good length of hair to hold on to, which is why they are particularly numerous in the winter when the coat is longest. The adult female lays about 20-30 eggs (or nits) every one to two days during her life and glues them onto the hair with a sticky secretion. After a few days, the eggs hatch and a tiny version of the adult louse emerges which moults a couple of times before reaching its adult size and state. Equine lice are host specific – they cannot survive on humans or other animals – and are passed from pony to pony by direct contact. Infestations are easily treated with louse powder; this should be applied twice, with a 10-day interval (in order to kill off new emergents from the nits). But first catch your pony ...!

Ponies play host to a variety of ticks, especially in warm weather: small black or cream ones can be found on the head, especially on the nose, and larger, cream coloured ones are found on the lower parts of the body and at the top of the legs. In Britain and other temperate areas, ticks are not believed to cause a pony much discomfort or harm, but in hotter climates they can carry infection and cause anaemia. Lyme disease, an infection carried by some ticks and transmissible to humans, through sheep and deer ticks, has not been confirmed in ponies, although the organism involved has been found in horses in the USA.

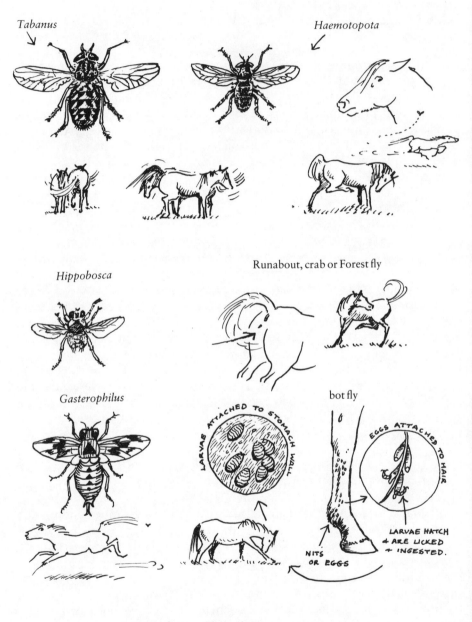

Tabanus

Haemotopota

Hippobosca

Runabout, crab or Forest fly

Gasterophilus

bot fly

LARVAE ATTACHED TO STOMACH WALL

EGGS ATTACHED TO HAIR

NITS OR EGGS

LARVAE HATCH & ARE LICKED & INGESTED.

Flying visitors.

Flying visitors

Midges are abundant in wet areas from May to September in the early morning and evening. Most ponies are not particularly bothered by them, but some react badly to the bite of one of the common species, *Culicoides pulicaris,* which feeds amongst the hairs of the mane and tail. An allergic reaction to the saliva of this midge is thought to cause the condition known as 'sweet itch', in which a sensitive pony rubs away the hairs of the mane and tail, often to the extent that the skin becomes damaged and infected. The sensitivity associated with sweet itch is thought to be hereditary and many owners selectively cull ponies which are susceptible.

During the summer and autumn, ponies are plagued by flies, which can cause and spread infection, although ponies probably suffer most from the irritation and discomfort that they cause. In order to gain some relief, ponies carry out 'comfort' behaviours of twitching the skin (they can shake off a fly from their skin by the localized involuntary contraction of a muscle lying under the skin), tail-swishing, stamping, rolling and moving. This constant activity interferes with ponies' normal feeding and resting patterns, which can cause a loss of condition.

There are two types of true horsefly in Britain: the large (up to 2.5 cm long), yellow and brown *Tabanus,* and the smaller (1-1.5 cm long), mottled brown, cigar-shaped *Haematopota.* Both are blood-suckers and cause much annoyance to ponies wherever they occur. They feed by cutting away the pony's skin with scissor-like mouthparts and sucking the blood out of the cut. Needless to say this is very painful for a pony, and can result in quite a substantial loss of blood. Most ponies become very agitated when a horsefly approaches and try to prevent it landing by tail-flicking, stamping, head shaking and, in some cases, running away. A case has been reported of a horse running into a fence and dying as a result of fly attack.

In the New Forest and parts of Dartmoor, the ponies have a third fly to contend with: *Hippobosca equina* – known locally as the 'run-about', 'crab fly' or 'forest fly'. It is smaller than the other horseflies (about 1 cm long) and is particularly well designed for its parasitic lifestyle with a flattened body and large, gripping claws, together with a startling ability to run sideways as well as backwards and forwards. Once it has landed on a pony it usually takes up residence between the back legs or under the tail where it is almost impossible for it to be dislodged. It is a blood-sucking fly and, although it causes discomfort to its host, most local ponies seem to tolerate it and accept the futility of attempting to dislodge it, although newcomers to crab fly areas find it extremely irritating. To date, it appears to be confined to just the two areas, and is a relatively recent arrival on Dartmoor where it only occurs in certain parts.

In addition to these blood-suckers, ponies are plagued in summer by the face fly *Musca autumnalis*. A close relative of the house fly, it feeds on secretions around the eyes, nose and mouth, and any blood which may be available from injuries or horsefly bites.

The botflies, *Gasterophilus nasalis* and *G. intestinalis*, lay their yellow eggs on a pony's coat in late summer and early autumn but do not bite or suck blood. *G. nasalis* lays on the lower jaw and *intestinalis* lays anywhere else on the body where it cannot be knocked off, such as the chest, neck and forelegs. The eggs are harmless, but the larvae hatch out to become internal parasites. The larvae of *G. nasalis* hatch whilst still on the coat and migrate into the mouth and then down to the stomach. *G. intestinalis* larvae hatch out after a pony has licked them off the coat whilst grooming or allogrooming (see page 51). They also spend time in the mouth and then pass down to the stomach and lower gut. Botfly larvae grow to about 1.5 cm long and cause irritation and some ulceration of the tongue, gums and gut, but they are not thought to cause the pony serious harm.

In the past, the name 'botfly' has been used for the warble fly *Hypoderma bovis* which also lays its eggs on horses and cattle. The eggs create sores which enable the larvae to burrow under the skin as they hatch. They stay under the skin for a few days after which they bore their way out and pupate elsewhere before emerging as adults. A pony with 'warbles' has lumps on its back about the size of small walnuts. Cattle are more prone to warbles than horses and, due to stringent methods of control applied to cattle since the 1970s, they are now very rare in horses.

Why do ponies stand in the middle of the road?

Do *they want to be traffic wardens?*

Do *they like exhaust fumes?*

Are *they latent jay-walkers?*

No, *the answer is simple – flies. This summertime behaviour, known as 'shading', also occurs in* the middle of an open plain and on the top of a hill and, despite its name, does not necessarily include an area of shade (some ponies will take to the woods or the shade of buildings in hot weather but these areas may contain other types of irritating fly). Flies are most active in warm, sunny, calm conditions and they need vegetation on which to settle after a large blood meal. In unvegetated and exposed areas where there is a breeze their numbers are lower. Ponies use the same places for shading every summer and they have no qualms about holding up the traffic or blocking the path to the ice cream van. Roads are especially popular because of the breeze that the passing cars create; exhaust fumes may also help to reduce fly attack.

Several groups of ponies may join together to shade, and it is not unusual to see over fifty ponies resting close together during the heat of the day. Research in the Camargue, where tabanid horseflies are a particular problem, has shown that horses in larger groups had fewer flies on them, and therefore fewer bites, than those in smaller groups. Ponies in large groups are better able to knock flies off each other and, with so many horses in one area, the number of flies per horse is likely to be lower than it would be for fewer individuals.

Lodgers inside

Most of a pony's internal lodgers are nematode and cestode worms – the roundworms, pinworms and tapeworms – the botfly larvae described above are something of an exception. Internal lodgers are potentially far more damaging to a pony's health than those that live outside, and heavy infestations can lead to permanent damage of body tissues.

The adults of most pony worms live in the intestines of their hosts where they feed, usually on blood or faecal matter, and produce eggs. The eggs are passed out with the dung and another (or the same) pony picks up the infection by eating contaminated vegetation. Although ponies do not normally feed close to their own dung in order to avoid eating parasite eggs (see page 69), the eggs of some parasites hatch in the dung or on the ground, and the infective larvae move away from the immediate area in droplets of water on the vegetation.

Ponies carry their highest burden of adult worms in spring, when larvae that have laid dormant in the pony over the winter develop into adults and larvae that have been dormant on vegetation also begin to develop. This mass emergence of adult worms in a pony's gut can cause it to suffer chronic diarrhoea and weight loss, which in extreme cases can be fatal. The adult worm population also increases at times of stress and trauma when the pony's immune system is incapacitated, such as during late, pregnancy, giving birth, lactation and bacterial and viral infections. The worms produce most eggs in autumn when their host is in good condition (see page 84).

Roundworms are the most damaging to a pony's health, especially the large redworms of the strongyle family (*Strongylus* spp.) and, in young ponies, the large (25-50 cm long) ascarid worm *Parascaris equorum*. When adult, both these worms damage the gut by slashing the wall and sucking blood, and the redworms are a common cause of colic. In their larval stages both can cause lasting damage to the tissues of the blood vessels and liver as they migrate around the body. *Parascaris* larvae also pass through the lungs and are a common cause of coughing in young ponies. These roundworms can bring about the death of their host if present in large numbers. A young pony can die if its gut becomes blocked or ruptured by *Parascaris,* and the redworms can cause a major loss in body condition which renders the pony vulnerable to other infections. Ponies can also carry many hundreds of small strongyle worms (Cyathostomes); these are less harmful to the pony than their larger relatives but they can cause persistent diarrhoea.

WORM YOUR DOGS !

The pinworm *Oxyuris equi* and the tapeworms, *Anoplocephala perfoliata and Paranoplocephala mamillana,* are also frequently encountered in a pony's gut but, although they are quite large worms (both tapeworms can be over 10 cm long), they are believed to cause less harm to the pony than the roundworms. Ponies become infected by pinworms by eating the eggs which then hatch out in the intestines. Adult pinworms lay their eggs around the pony's anus, causing much irritation to the pony who rubs its tail against any convenient tree or post, and by so doing rubs the eggs off and onto the ground. Although ponies may carry several hundred pinworms, unlike the roundworms, they are not considered to be particularly harmful, although excessive rubbing of the tail can result in local infection of the damaged skin. Ponies normally only carry a few tapeworms, which are acquired from the accidental consumption of free-living mites infected with the larvae. These lodgers have little effect on their host, but large numbers of *A. perfoliata* can cause chronic diarrhoea. Ponies also play host to the larval ('hydatid') cyst stage of the dog tapeworm *Echinococcus granulosus equinus,* acquired from eggs passed out with dog faeces. The cysts appear as swellings in the liver which can be several centimetres in diameter and filled with fluid. Although large, the cyst is not thought to cause the pony serious harm, but there is growing concern about this infection, which is becoming more common in British pony populations.

Help?

These internal lodgers can be treated with orally administered drugs ('wormers' or 'anthelmintics') but, like vaccinations, they are expensive and should be given a number of times during the year. Although the recommendation is every 6-8 weeks, recent research in the New Forest has shown that if ponies are only wormed once a year this still has some effect, by reducing their internal worm population and so improving their body condition. If only a single dose is available it is best given in the autumn, which is fortunately the time when many ponies are rounded up. If worms are removed at this time, when most eggs are produced, the burden of adults that the pony would have to carry through the winter and the number of eggs on the ground to reinfect others are reduced. Most eggs and larvae do not survive hot, dry, sunny conditions, and on hot, sunny days breaking up dung piles by harrowing also helps to reduce reinfection.

It is often suggested that free-ranging ponies are not as vulnerable to major infestations of internal parasites as their domestic counterparts because they are not confined to a small area. This is not necessarily the

case. I described earlier how ponies live within a given area or home range (see page 42); within this area there are usually certain habitats that they prefer for feeding over others, for example open grassland. Many ponies congregate on such preferred areas, especially from spring to autumn, and the grazing pressure and consequent chance of parasitic infection is high. Levels of internal parasitic infection have been measured in some populations and they are usually found to be clinically high, despite the fact that many ponies range in areas grazed by cattle or sheep. There is evidence that ponies possess a certain amount of natural tolerance towards their internal lodgers (see below).

Vaccinations and medications are valuable sources of prevention and cure but free-ranging ponies have to be found and caught in order to receive them. In Britain many ponies are caught at annual round-ups and may be treated then, but at other times this requires considerable time and effort from the owner, first to find and then to catch the animal. Sick ponies tend to hide themselves somewhere quiet and out of the way. However, ponies have survived and thrived for many thousands of years without man's help and employ a number of their own natural remedies.

Immunity and resistance

After an infection, an animal usually acquires a certain amount of immunity to reinfection. For ponies, this is the case for diseases such as strangles and, to a lesser extent, 'flu, and infestations of some of the internal parasites, for example *Parascaris equorum*, which is rarely found in ponies aged over two years. In general, mature ponies aged over four years maintain lower levels of internal parasite infestation than young ponies.

Resistance to disease and infection is likely to be hereditary. Ponies from unmanaged populations where only the fittest survive to breed and pass on their genes are likely to be more resistant than those from managed populations where selection pressures are different.

Natural medicines

It has been suggested that some plants act as natural wormers (vermifuges). Claims have been made for gorse, ling *(Calluna vulgaris)*, plants of salty areas and spring grass; the latter can certainly purge a pony of some of its parasites. Bracken may also have vermifuge properties, which might explain why ponies eat it despite its being toxic and having little or no nutritional value. No detailed scientific studies on the worming properties of any of these plants have been carried out, so far as I am aware.

Helpers

Wild ungulates in Africa, including zebras, receive help from oxpeckers in removing external parasites. These birds are specialized for clinging onto the pelts of the animals and removing ticks in particular. Other birds, for example starlings, jackdaws and magpies in Britain, and starlings, redwinged blackbirds, cattle egrets and cattle tyrants elsewhere perform similar tasks for ponies. Ponies also help each other by standing tail-swishing nose to tail and by allogrooming.

Ponies and people

Mounts in Alexander the Great's day (c. 338 BC) were probably small ponies.

Man and horse led overlapping lives for many thousands of years. To begin with the horse was a source of food and later it became a means of transport and an aid to agriculture; its development for primarily recreational purposes is relatively recent. Some 30,000 years ago Eurasian man hunted horses for meat. The cave drawings of Lascaux in the Dordogne, southern France and Altamira Caves at Santillana del Mar, northern Spain, suggest that the practice spread to western Europe as well. Domestication is believed to have first occurred some time between 4,000 and 3,000 BC in Eurasia; we do not know either where or when for certain, and it may have occurred in several places at more or less the same time. One theory is that horses were first tamed in the steppes somewhere between Hungary and Manchuria, and that the skill gradually spread out west to Britain and south to North Africa by about 3,000 BC. It is probable that at first horses were used as pack animals and for driving, but there is hieroglyph evidence of horses used for riding in Egypt in about 2,000 BC. The first domestic horses were in fact probably ponies. Boadicea's chariot would more likely have been drawn by animals resembling today's Exmoor ponies rather than the fiery stallions of popular imagination. The horses carved on the Parthenon friezes, and William the Conqueror's horses shown on the Bayeux Tapestry, were also probably ponies if we judge from the relative size of their riders, who would themselves have been smaller in those times than today's men and women.

Folklore and religion

Because of man's close links with horses, it is not surprising to find that they feature in many myths and legends. In many cultures, horses are portrayed as gods: here are a few examples from around the world.

For the ancient Greeks the horse represented perfect movement and musical rhythm. It also symbolized wave motion as the chariot of Poseidon (who was believed to have created the horse) was drawn by horses from the sea into the air. Pegasus, the most famous of all winged horses, was the steed of the sun god Apollo and was believed to have created the Hippocrene Fountain where he stamped his hoof on Mount Helicon (Central Greece).

In Islam, Al Borak was the animal brought by Gabriel to carry Mohammed to the seventh heaven, and was itself received into Paradise. It had the face of a man and the cheeks of a horse, with eyes like jacinths, but brilliant as the stars; it had the wings of an eagle, spoke with the voice of a man and glittered all over with radiant light. A mosque stands at the point where it leapt from earth up to heaven.

In Scandinavian mythology, Skinfaxi ('shining mane') is the horse of the day and his counterpart by night is Hrimfaxi ('frost mane') from whose bit fall the drops of rime which cover the earth by night. Sleipnir is the eight-footed horse of the god Odin; he can cross land and sea alike, and his eight legs stand for the eight main points from which the wind blows.

The Gauls and Celts worshipped the goddess Epona amongst other deities. The name means 'great mare'. Originally a spirited horse-goddess of fruitfulness, she later became a human goddess and protector of horses and mules, always in the company of horses and usually riding a mare and feeding a foal. In Wales she is known as Rhianon. In England, the white horse was the emblem of the Saxons. This may or may not be the reason for some of the white horses carved in chalk hillsides in parts of southern England. The famous one at Uffington in Berkshire is traditionally said to commemorate Alfred the Great's victory over the Danes in 871. In more recent times, a galloping white horse was the device of the royal House of Hanover and, during the reigns of George I and II 'The White Horse' replaced 'The Royal Oak' of Stuart fame on many inn-signs.

The commoners

In Britain, all ponies are owned and populations are tightly managed; this gives a much closer association with man than exists in the western US or Australia. Ownership carries its own sub-culture and a seasonal cycle of activities for the owners and local people.

Owners are responsible for the welfare of their stock, but this is easier said than done when dealing with the canny mentality of the average pony who will not be found when you want it and cannot be caught with a bucket and headcollar! In most areas individual owners or 'commoners' (so called because they run their stock on the moor or Forest by a common right of pasture attached to their properties) co-operate (personalities permitting), and in areas with large populations of ponies, such as the New Forest, Dartmoor and Wales, Commoners' Associations exist, which provide a means of co-ordinating major management operations such as round-ups (see below).

In the New Forest, in addition to a Commoners' Association, there are five men whose job it is to oversee the welfare of the stock and inform owners of any problems. These are the 'agisters' – the name is mediaeval and originated from officers of the Crown who collected and accounted for money charged for the right to graze stock, known as the 'agistment'. Agisters are employed by the Court of Verderers, a group of five appointed and five elected people which shares the administration of the Forest with the Crown (Forestry Commission) and represents the interests of the commoners. The agisters are partially funded by the marking fee which owners pay per animal turned out (£15 per head for ponies in 1993). The Forest is divided into four districts; the head agister oversees the whole area and the other four look after a district each. Their duties range from collecting marking fees to attending road traffic accidents which involve Forest stock, and they may be called out at any time of day or night. Quick-thinking and surgical skills are an advantage, as this excerpt from an agister's diary shows:

May 20th
...Totton for animal food. Home. Call to Ashurst Hospital*, mare having foaling problems. Attended and studied situation. Mare had

(*Note: Ashurst Hospital does not have a pony maternity unit – the mare in question was on a Forest lawn close by).

foaled an hour or so before I was called, but the foal was still attached to the umbilical cord. Scrounged thread and sterilizing fluid from Hospital, tied off cord and cut it. Foal very weak so left it to lay in the sun and gain strength. Home. Call from police, return to Ashurst, someone had called the vet. Returned, met vet, nothing left for her to do. Home but returned later, foal now on its feet. Home.

A certain degree of patience, tolerance and good humour are also essential for the job – particularly where ponies like 'Sooty', an old black mare with a liking for gardens, was concerned:

January 4th
...11.50 p.m. call from Woodlands, pony in garden. Attended and returned 'Sooty' to Forest. It seems she has perfected the art of opening the wicket gate by the grid if the wire loop is left up.

January 11th
...Home to message about 'Sooty' being out again at Woodlands. Attended and modified gate catches once more.

February 13th
...Woodlands Road, to catch and move 'Sooty' who has been making herself unpopular getting into gardens. Managed to lure mare into Alpine Road with some hay, but as soon as she heard the lorry she was away.

April 5th
...Called at Woodlands Road. More complaints about 'Sooty', walking over the grid this time.

Much to the relief of some local residents 'Sooty' was eventually removed from the Forest and took a well earned retirement in her owner's field.

An agister's life used to be even more eventful before the New Forest was fenced in the early 1960s, at which time cattle-grids were also installed. The ponies could roam for miles and it was not unusual to have to retrieve them from more than ten miles beyond the official boundary. Southampton to the east, Wimborne to the west and the out-

skirts of Salisbury to the north all harboured vagrant ponies at one time and another. In the days before the agisters and owners had motor transport, recovery must have been particularly arduous with just bicycles and ponies to rely on. A pony like 'Sooty' would certainly have been one of the many 'lane creepers' which spread out from the Forest along the lanes and spent their lives in and out of gardens. Some ponies were particularly artful and would only go into gardens at night, returning to their usual daytime haunts by dawn as if they had never been away.

Today, boundaries and main roads are fenced and gridded and the agisters have vehicles and mobile telephones, but the ponies are just as smart; they can roll over cattle grids, find holes in fences and, like 'Sooty', open gates.

Elsewhere, there are no such official bodies and the commoners oversee their own stock, although on Dartmoor there is a group of volunteers, the Dartmoor Livestock Protection Society, who look after the welfare of ponies, cattle and sheep on the moor. They are supported by farmers and the Dartmoor Commoners' Council and have their own rescue service which can be called on at any time and, if necessary, will pay vets' bills.

Which is whose?

Some ponies can be identified by their appearance; they may be an unusual colour or shape or have distinctive white marks. However, there are also many plain bays, greys and browns, and with Exmoor ponies distinctive marks are simply not allowed. Although many owners 'know' their ponies, in order to avoid confusion and arguments an objective form of identification is necessary. In many areas this is achieved by ...

Branding

With the exception of Exmoors the brand is made up of letters, numbers or symbols of the owner's choice – often his or her initials. Exmoor ponies have the pony society star-shaped brand on their shoulders, but they cannot be branded with this until they have been inspected and passed for registration by two breed society inspectors. If the pony has any white hairs in its coat or any conformational deformities, such as poorly aligned teeth, it cannot be registered. Registered Exmoors are individually identified by a herd number on the shoulder below the star and an individual number within that herd on the quarters, unless the pony belongs to the 'Anchor' herd of Winsford Common, when it has an anchor and an individual number on the quarters.

Hot branding is quick and the pony seems to suffer little if any discomfort.

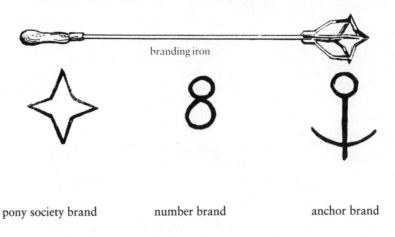

branding iron

pony society brand   number brand   anchor brand

Exmoor brands.

Ponies are hot branded, for which the branding iron is heated up until it is nearly white hot and applied firmly for one or two seconds to a specially clipped area of the pony's coat, usually on the shoulder, behind the withers or on the quarters. The operation produces a lot of smoke and a smell of burning but if the brand is hot enough the pony does not appear to suffer much, if any, discomfort. Most are more distressed about the restraint that they are under than the branding. I have seen tame ponies continue to eat from their hay nets whilst being branded and 'wild' ponies begin grazing immediately they are released. Some owners put grease on a fresh brand to help it heal, but ungreased brands seem to heal just as well. Branding is a skilled job and is only carried out by agisters and experienced commoners. Traditions have developed connected with branding. On Exmoor, the irons are heated up in the fire in the house and carried (at speed) out to the yard in a bucket of hot coals, while in the New Forest the brands are always heated up in a wood fire built near to where the branding is to take place (which can pose a few problems on wet days).

Ear marking
An alternative way of identifying a pony is by marking its ears. Ear marks in the form of nicks, holes and small metal or plastic tags are commonly used in Wales and on Dartmoor. Elsewhere many owners are reluctant to use this type of marking because of the risk of tetanus (see Disease), but I am not aware that this is a problem with the ear-marked Welsh Mountain ponies and Dartmoors.

Fire brands or freezers

In recent years, for humane reasons, there has been pressure to freeze-brand ponies with irons super-cooled in liquid nitrogen rather than to hot-brand them. Freeze-branding is commonly used for security marking domestic horses and now, by law, has to be used for cattle, but its use is being strongly resisted for free-ranging ponies. The most stressful thing about branding for 'wild' ponies is the restraint required. Hot-branding requires the pony to be still for just one or two seconds, whereas at least thirty seconds' immobility is required for a freeze-brand to be successful. Holding a pony completely still for such a length of time would not only be very difficult but, more importantly, it would greatly increase the stress caused to the pony compared to that caused by hot-branding.

'So that's who I am.'

Rounding up

Ponies are usually rounded up ('drifted' in the New Forest and on Dartmoor, 'gathered' on Exmoor and in Wales) once a year in the autumn, and in some parts of Dartmoor ponies are drifted again in January to remove any in poor condition. The ponies are not all rounded up at once; there are a number of drifts centred on particular areas. In the New Forest, about forty drifts take place from August to the beginning of November.

Drifts and gatherings are organized by the agisters in the New Forest and by owners and commoners' associations elsewhere. Owners, interested locals and the occasional tourist gather, on foot and on horseback, at a designated location near to the pound, yard or field into which the ponies are to be driven. A strategy is decided, walkers are allocated positions to help block roads, gaps in fences and vegetation and, particularly important, close the gate after the ponies have passed through, and the riders leave in search of the first group to be brought in. Relaxed conversation ensues amongst the walkers until the first rumble of hooves or cries of 'Look up!' are heard when ponies and riders suddenly seem to appear from nowhere. On a good day the ponies trot or canter obligingly though the gateway (especially if it appears to lead into a large grassy field) but there are many individuals who are less amenable and will try and turn back or break through the smallest gap in the defences, and you can be sure that it is these ponies that the owner particularly wants! It usually takes at least two drives to bring in the ponies from an area but it can take more where the ponies are widely dispersed or especially wily. On Exmoor where there are very few commoners who turn out ponies, the ponies are normally driven onto their owner's holding rather than into a communal pound or field.

As soon as the animals are impounded, the big sort-out begins. The ponies are held in a large pound, which may be a field or yard, and groups are brought into a smaller area. On Dartmoor and the New Forest all unbranded ponies which are to stay on the Forest or moor are branded, and in Wales unmarked ponies have their ears marked or tagged. In the New Forest, mares' and foals' tails are cut in a particular arrangement according to the district in which the owner lives; ponies of district 4, for example, have the right side of their tails cut short. Stallions' tails are cut straight. In other areas, such as Wales and Exmoor, some owners cut the tail in a particular shape to enable them to identify their ponies more easily from a distance and, in areas susceptible to heavy snowfalls, the tail is often cut to hock height to prevent it dragging on the ground and gathering snow – which can literally weigh the pony down. Hooves are trimmed if necessary and ponies are wormed if the owner chooses. Since 1990, wormers (one per pony) have been provided free of charge in the New Forest by the Verderers with the help of a grant from the International League for the Protection of Horses. Once all this has been done, the ponies not going for sale are released onto the moor or Forest, although animals in particularly poor condition are usually taken to a field or yard where they can receive extra food in order to improve in condition before they are released. Ponies that are to be sold are not usually tail-marked or wormed and are transported to the owner's holding where they are held until the sale. It is illegal to sell foals aged less than four months without their dams. Exmoor ponies may be kept on the owner's holding for a few days, especially if they are

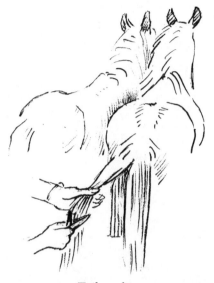

Tail marking.

unbranded and have to wait for inspection by the breed society.

Blood samples taken from ponies at New Forest drifts have been analysed for biochemical signs of stress and have shown that this hectic activity is not stressful for the animals. This is more than can be said for some of the owners; I am reliably informed that in the not-so-distant past, fights over ownership of ponies were not uncommon at some drifts! Today, matters are better regulated – or perhaps the lunches are less liquid – and, although there is an important job of work to be done, the drifts and gatherings offer a good opportunity to meet and talk and are an important event in the commoners' calendar. Sometimes there are even rewards for turning out; there is a drift on Dartmoor at which all the participants receive pasties and beer at lunchtime (I am not telling where!) and it is not unknown for hot-dogs (complete with all the trimmings) to appear at the last New Forest drift of the season. On Exmoor the 'brandings' are held on the holdings and this too can be an enjoyable social occasion, sometimes including an excellent tea.

A number of local sales are held each autumn in Wales, the New Forest and on Dartmoor. At Llandovery and Brecon Fairs, for example, Welsh Mountain ponies from the hill are presented for sale (the lowland and stud ponies usually go to the Fayre Oaks sale at Hereford market), sales of New Forest ponies take place once a month from August to December at

Ponies are rounded up by a group of riders ...

... and brought into a small pound where they are sorted out.

Beaulieu Road, and Tavistock market is a popular venue for the sale of Dartmoor ponies. In some areas there are additional sales in the spring.

Sales are inevitably very stressful for ponies, and for many foals it is their first day away from their mothers. Ponies are brought to the sales in lorries or trailers (in the past they were driven there by mounted drovers) and are unloaded into small pens, where they are held in small groups. Stallions are put in separate pens. The ponies are brought into the sale ring one at a time, the bidding begins, and when the pony is sold it goes to another pen from which it will be claimed by its new owner.

In recent years, the Ministry of Agriculture, Fisheries and Food (MAFF) has introduced a number of guidelines and laws in order to improve conditions for ponies at sales. For example, ponies which are lame, unwell, deformed, emaciated, thin or exhausted cannot be entered in the sale (an owner may be prosecuted for bringing them); clean, fresh water must be available in troughs or buckets so that animals may drink at least every eight hours (or more frequently in hot weather), foals must have suitable bedding (such as straw), and the fencing in the sale yard and pens must be of solid construction and in good condition to prevent breakouts or injury to ponies or handlers. Few ponies are halter-broken when they come to the sale and they have to be encouraged to move round the sale yard and ring by someone walking behind them; waving arms, a flag or a stick are permitted to help in this, but it is forbidden by law to hit or prod a pony at a sale. Local Authority inspectors are responsible for enforcing these regulations and, at most sales, there is also a veterinary surgeon and an RSPCA officer in attendance. On Exmoor there is no longer a local sale for the ponies and most owners sell from their holdings. Exmoor ponies, even the foals, can be very strong in body and mind, and handling them usually requires the same of their handlers – together with much patience.

'I'm staying here.'

Ponies at sales are not normally halter broken.

Why keep ponies?

They cost money, take time and cause heartache, so why do people do it? For many owners keeping ponies is a way of life that has been in the family for generations. Some gain much pleasure from showing and breaking in their better animals, just as others enjoy the knowledge that their ponies are out there – somewhere – and that they are helping to keep an ancient tradition alive. There is little if any profit to be made from running ponies and, if the time involved is costed, a substantial deficit is inevitable.

Many owners come under harsh criticism for the way in which they 'keep' their ponies. This is often ill-informed and derived from the human perception that a happy horse is one which is fat and tucked up in a stable. Anyone who has attempted to confine an untamed pony will know that this is not its natural, happy state. Ponies that are free-ranging are free from stable vices – stereotyped behaviour such as crib-biting and wind-sucking brought about by extreme boredom. They are able to range where they please and associate freely with other ponies.

However, some ponies do suffer in their free-ranging life; they may become ill or injured, or they may not be of a sufficiently hardy type to fend for themselves. It is not always possible to find a pony when you want to, especially a sick one which tends to hide away somewhere quiet, but most owners keep reasonable track of their animals, especially the more vulnerable ones such as the young and the old, and will respond if one is reported in trouble. But there are a few who do not. These people not only cause unnecessary suffering to their animals but they also give the other owners a bad name. Sometimes they are brought to task, but it is very difficult to prove negligence of a free-ranging pony. Some of the animals that belong to such people are fortunately found and helped by members of volunteer welfare organizations and charities who devote much time and effort to looking out for ponies in distress or in very poor condition. Such organizations exist throughout the country and many have their own horse transport and will pay vets' fees.

One man's meat

Ponies in Britain are not bred for meat, although inevitably some are sold for this purpose. At the moment most of the carcases are sold in Britain for pet food, and it must be said that this is a way of weeding out the weaker, less well conformed stock from the population. There are strict laws regarding the transport and slaughter of ponies in Britain to ensure that this is carried out as humanely as possible. Horses and ponies are not exported live from Britain for slaughter; under the terms of the 'Minimum Values Order' it is illegal to export live horses or ponies valued below a certain threshold equivalent to carcase value. Since most Continentals prefer their horsemeat 'on the hoof', relatively little British horsemeat is exported for human consumption. There was pressure from the Continent to repeal the Order with the opening of the European free market in 1992, but at the time of writing (1993) the Order still exists, due substantially to the combined efforts of British welfare organizations and the public.

Ponies for sale

Ponies of all ages are sold at sales, but in the autumn most are foals. If you know what you are doing, you can pick up a bargain. If you do not and are without the committed support of someone who does, don't do it!

- *Most ponies at sales have received little or no handling.*

Some owners halter break their foals before the sale, which usually raises the price and makes the sale process less of a struggle for owner and buyer, and minimizes stress for the pony.

- *If buying a pony to run on the Forest or moor, find out about* its ability to fend for itself; if the parents do well then the foal is likely to follow suit. If buying a mare that you want to breed from, make sure that she has foaled (many mares are sold because they have not).

- A young foal is an attractive and endearing creature. This on its own is not a sound reason for buying one. Remember that it will be at least three years and a lot of hard work before you begin to ride or drive it, or a filly will have her first foal.
- If buying a colt, add on the cost of having it gelded – unless you want a stallion.
- If you are interested in showing, buy a stud book registered pony or one eligible for registration. Such a pony may be more expensive, but it has a documented identity, is eligible to enter breed and mountain and moorland classes and its resale value is likely to be higher.
- A pony has been used to the companionship of other members of its group from birth. Removal from this situation to one of isolation and confinement is traumatic and stressful, especially for foals – many of which have only been weaned on the morning of the sale. An equine companion can help a pony to adjust to its new environment.

- After purchase, the pony should be wormed (unless this has only just been done) and it is a good idea to vaccinate against tetanus – young foals are notorious for getting into trouble in unfamiliar surroundings.

- Do not allow your pony to overeat on good pasture. This can lead to laminitis, a crippling and painful inflammation of the lamina tissues inside the hoof which is caused by obesity. Free-ranging ponies do not suffer from this but adults brought into captivity are particularly susceptible when faced with an excess of rich food.

An ecological mowing machine

In recent years there has been a growing trend in Britain and Europe to manage grassland with grazing animals in order to prevent the encroachment of scrub and unwanted coarse grasses. The Dutch were among the first to do this and much of their reclaimed grassland is currently maintained by Konig ponies – which have been found to be much hardier than cattle. In wetland areas such as the Camargue, the estuary of the River Seine (northern France) and the saltmarshes of the Dutch Friesland islands (northern Netherlands), grazing by horses and ponies has helped to maintain a high species diversity and richness within the plant communities, and to preserve open marshland for water birds by preventing the encroachment of reed beds.

In Britain, the idea is spreading. In 1989 New Forest ponies were 'invited' to graze certain areas of National Trust land in Hampshire, Wiltshire and the Isle of Wight. In 1990 six Exmoor ponies were bought by the National Trust to graze an area of grassland in Purbeck, Dorset. Three years later, there is a stallion with nine mares and four foals and, because the grass has been kept short through grazing, the rare early spider orchid (*Ophrys sphegodes*) and the bee orchid (*O. apifera*) are flowering in the area once again. In autumn 1992 another six Exmoor mares were released onto the Quantock Hills in Somerset, where Exmoor ponies last lived about 1,000 years ago. In less than a year violets have returned to the tracks and the deer are more numerous; a foal was born in April. And in 1993 twenty Exmoor ponies were despatched to Cornwall where they are keeping down invading scrub vegetation on Breney Common and Red Moor Reserve near Bodmin.

Please don't feed the ponies, for your sake ...

- Ponies have sharp teeth and heels and will chase after you and your food. When they are accustomed to being fed they can turn very nasty if they are refused; a small child is a vulnerable target for a spoilt, greedy pony.
- They are not afraid to enter tents and awnings uninvited – not only will they readily eat what is there but they are untidy animals and do not move carefully in confined spaces ...
- Do not feel sorry for them. They have plenty of natural food to eat.

... and for theirs

- Most human food is not suitable for ponies. It can cause colic, with ensuing great pain and possible death for the ponies. Foals are particularly vulnerable owing to their natural curiosity and they may eat plastic litter as well as your picnic. This can lead to illness and sometimes death.

- Camp sites, car parks and picnic areas do not offer much natural food for ponies because of the trampling that these areas receive, so ponies that spend most of their time in these places do not eat well.

- Feeding ponies at roadsides encourages them to wait there for food and so increases their chances of being hit by a motor vehicle. Again, foals are particularly vulnerable.

People as pests

An all too common occurrence.

I described earlier the common ailments and injuries that ponies suffer during their free-ranging life (see pp. 90-92). Ponies are remarkably tough and most live and breed unaided by man. Often it is the presence of man that causes disease and injury; man drops litter, leaves fence wire where it can become caught around ponies' legs and feeds ponies with unsuitable food, but above all he drives a car. In Britain motor vehicles are responsible for more pony deaths than any other single factor.

The New Forest, Dartmoor, Exmoor and some of the Welsh hills are crossed by busy roads and accidents are common. In the New Forest, which is one of the worst areas for pony road deaths, over 100 ponies are killed on the roads each year, with a further 20–30 injured. Despite the heavy tourist pressure here and on the moors, it is not tourists but local people who cause most of the accidents. The main culprits are people who cross the Forest or moor on a regular basis and are over-familiar with the route. No matter how well you may know the road, you can never know for sure what a pony is going to do next. Particularly appalling is the number of drivers who do not stop, or at the very least report the accident. They are too afraid of the price they will have to pay for the animal or perhaps they were over the legal alcohol limit. As a result of their callousness, many ponies are left to suffer horribly for hours until they are found – often with one, or even two, broken legs. It is a criminal offence to fail to stop and report an accident where damage is caused.

Efforts have been made to reduce accidents in the New Forest and on Dartmoor, especially on high risk roads. Initially, large, bright signs were erected at intervals along the road – 'Watch Out! Animals About!' Although quite striking to newcomers and tourists, they rapidly lost their impact to frequent users of the roads. Suggestions to fence the vulnerable roads have been rejected because this would reduce the grazing area available to the ponies and other animals, and the provision of an adequate number of underpasses so that ponies could still get to the grazing would be too expensive.

It is generally accepted that a reduction of speed reduces the number of accidents. 'Sleeping policeman' cannot be installed because the roads are unlit, but rumble strips are permissible, and in 1987-88 some were laid down on busy roads on Dartmoor and the New Forest. These were not successful and in the New Forest, speeds of over 80 mph were recorded, and 60 mph (the legal limit at the time) was common. On Dartmoor the rumble strips remain, but in the New Forest they were removed and a series of new measures, initiated by Hampshire County Council, were tried along some of the busiest roads. These included a 40 mph speed limit, narrow 'pinch points' or chicanes, a different kind of rumble strip (designed to be very uncomfortable at speeds of over 30 mph), and special 'gateways' to some of the busiest roads crossing the Forest, with bold signs and a noisy, bumpy concrete lattice type of surface for about twenty metres after the cattle grid. After about a year the pinch points were removed since the bollards had become dented and bent after many speeding cars had bounced off them, and the 30 mph rumble strips were also removed owing to a fatal accident, despite rigorous safety testing. But these trials were not completely in vain; the 'gateways' remain and since 1992, all unfenced Forest roads have a speed limit of 40 mph. This limit has been successful in reducing animal deaths and is being considered for other areas where animals, usually sheep, graze on land abutting unfenced roads.

Most accidents occur in the dark when ponies are almost invisible except for their eyes, which shine in a car's headlights. There have been a number of attempts to make the animals more visible. Some years ago, reflective red discs were stuck on the ponies' rumps; the ponies could be seen more easily, but unfortunately a number of drivers mistook them for roadside markers and followed them off the road! More recently, reflective neck bands were tried on ponies in parts of Dartmoor and the New Forest and, although the ponies were more visible, most had lost their neckbands within a month. It is difficult to think of alternative

Reflective ponies – not such a good idea.

parts of a pony where a reflective band or tag could be fastened securely and safely, without irritation to the animal. Reflective leg bands, for example, would fall off after their first journey through a bog or coarse, old heather. The idea of reflective clothing for ponies has therefore been shelved for the time being.

Despite all of these efforts, deaths on the roads are still unacceptably high. The police cannot be at every corner to catch speeding motorists, and whilst the route across the moor or the Forest continues to be the quickest and most direct, the load of traffic and, therefore, the number of deaths will increase. Perhaps the idea of one New Forest Commoner to turn all the forest roads to gravel is worth taking seriously ...

The future?

In most places where ponies live they are an attraction, bringing tourists and an income into the area. The New Forest or Dartmoor without ponies is unimaginable.

Many feral populations are under threat because they compete with domestic stock for resources, and managed populations are generally declining in number because of economic pressures on the owners. Low sale prices, loss of stock through road traffic accidents, cost of property and a lack of affordable back-up land on which to bring the ponies off common land should problems occur all contribute to this. Several of the British breeds, such as Exmoor, Dales and Eriskay ponies are now at such low numbers that they are registered with the Rare Breeds Survival Trust and most of the free-ranging populations have been lost from Europe. In some areas, such as the New Forest and Dartmoor, premium schemes to encourage the running of hardy stock of an appropriate type are in force and offer some assistance and encouragement to the owners. In Wales premiums are awarded to selected stallions to run out with mares owned by an Improvement Society on various specified hills and commons.

Our free-ranging ponies are an irreplaceable resource. The original hardy types have already been lost from many breeds and, if the resilience of those remaining is to be maintained, there must be a root stock to return to.

During the hundreds or even thousands of years that ponies have lived on the moors and forests, they have made a major contribution to the unique ecological condition of these areas today. Together with cattle, sheep and deer, they have ensured by their grazing and browsing that areas of moorland, heathland and hill have not become impassable jungles of scrub and coarse grasses.

It is likely that the original wild horse has now been lost to us. Today's non-feral free-ranging ponies represent some of the last remnants of the foundation stock from which many of the modern breeds originated, so providing a vital genetic resource for breeders of horses throughout the world, which must be maintained.

Further reading

There are many books about horses and ponies, most of which concentrate on how to look after and ride and show them, and describe the different breeds; I would not like to nominate any one definitive text in this category! Instead, I have listed below a few publications which relate more to free-ranging ponies, the areas in which they live and the biology of horses and ponies in general. Further, more detailed, scientific information may be obtained from the bibliographies of these publications.

Baker, S.E., *Survival of the Fittest; a Natural History of the Exmoor Pony* (Exmoor Books, Dulverton, Somerset, 1993)

Berger, J., *Wild Horses of the Great Basin* (Chicago University Press, 1986).

Christie, B.J., *The Horses of Sable Island* (Petheric Press Ltd., Halifax, Nova Scotia, Canada, 1980).

Clabby, J. *The Natural History of the Horse* (Weidenfield & Nicholson, London, 1976).

Duncan, P. (ed.), *Zebras, Asses and Horses. An Action Plan for the Conservation of Wild Equids* (IUCN Species Survival Commission, 1992).

Evans, J.W., A. Borton, H.F. Hintz & L.D. van Vleck, *The Horse* (W.H. Freeman & Co., New York, 2nd edition, 1990).

Gill, E.L., *Further Studies of Factors Affecting the Body Condition of Free-ranging Ponies* (RSPCA Scientific Publications, the Causeway, Horsham, West Sussex, 1991).

Keiper, R.R., *The Assateague Ponies* (Tidewater Publishers, Centreville, Maryland, USA, 1985).

Ponaidh Publications, *Going Native,* a quarterly publication obtainable by mail order from Ponaidh Publications, 12, Abbotsford, Bartley, Southampton, Hampshire, SO4 2LU.

Russell, V., *New Forest Ponies* (David & Charles, Newton Abbott, 1976).

Speed, J.G. & M.G., *The Exmoor Pony – its origins and characteristics* (Countrywide Livestock Ltd., Eastrip House, Colerne, Chippenham, Wiltshire, UK, 1977).

Tubbs, C.R., *The New Forest, a Natural History* (Collins, London, 1986).

Tyler, S.J., *The Behaviour and Social Organisation of the New Forest Ponies* (Animal Behaviour Monographs, 5(2): 85-196, 1972).

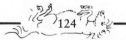

Glossary of biological and equine terms

Arab breed of small horse believed to have originated over 5,000 years ago in the deserts of the Middle East. Renowned for its soundness, endurance and grace, it has been involved in the 'improvement' of many other breeds.

Bay a colour in which the body is brown and the lower legs, mane, tail, tips of the ears and sometimes the end of the nose are black.

Break in to train a horse or pony to accept a saddle, bridle and rider or harness, cart and driver (see also 'halter break' below).

Brown dark brown all over the body and without the black markings of a bay (see above).

Cannon bone the large long bone of the lower leg; it is the metacarpus of the forelegs and metatarsus of the hind legs.

Chestnut a colour in which the body and legs are light to medium brown and the mane and tail can vary in shade from blonde to dark brown. Also the name given to a small horny patch on the inside of the upper front and lower hind legs; it may be a vestigial toe pad or the remnants of a scent gland.

Cob a stocky, short-legged pony or small horse.

Coloured pony or horse with patches of brown, black and white.

Colt uncastrated male aged less than four years.

Cones colour-sensitive cells in the eye.

Convergent evolution similarity between two organs or organisms which has arisen through independent evolution along similar lines, rather than as a result of having a common ancestor.

Cover the act of mating (copulation) by a stallion.

Dewlap a fold of loose skin hanging down from the throat.

Dun colour in which the body is a creamy yellow to sandy colour and the lower legs, mane, tail, ear tips and sometimes the end of the nose are black.

Filly a female aged less than four years.

Forekick the raising and kicking out of a foreleg, usually performed when meeting another individual, especially during sexual and stallion to stallion encounters.

Gelding a castrated male.

Goose rump where the rump slopes down steeply from its highest point to the top of the tail.

Grey a colour ranging from dark grey to white.

Halter break to train a horse or pony to accept the wearing and restraint of a headcollar or halter.

Hand unit of measurement of horses and ponies. 1 hand = 4 inches (10 cm). The number of inches between hands is expressed thus: 1 inch = .1; 2 inches = .2; 3 inches = .3. Height is measured from the ground to the withers (see below).

Hock large joint of the back leg between the tibia/fibula and cannon bone (metatarsus), made up of the tarsus, talus (tibial tarsal bone) and calcaneus (fibular tarsal bone).

Horse large type of *Equus caballus* of over 14.2 hands (145 cm) in height. Also used when referring to a stallion (regardless of height).

Knee large joint half way down the foreleg between the ulna/radius and the cannon bone (metacarpus), made up of the carpus in front with the accessory carpal bone behind. Not the same joint as a human knee.

Mare female horse or pony aged four years and over.

Palomino colour in which the body is golden to cream and the mane and tail are blonde.

Piebald colour of black and white patches.

Pony small type of *Equus caballus* of up to 14.2 hands (145 cm) in height.

Population collection of animals of the same species resident in the same area and which can usually be divided into a number of smaller social groups.

Quarters hind quarters, the rump and upper region of the hind legs.

Roan colour where the coat is flecked with white hairs throughout. For example, bay roan is bay with white hairs, strawberry roan is chestnut with white hairs.

Skewbald colour of brown and white patches.

Stallion uncastrated (entire) male horse or pony aged four years and over.

Territory defined area which the occupier actively defends.

Thoroughbred English breed of horse used for racing and other riding purposes whose ancestry can be traced to Weatherby's stud book Nos. 1-5, first published in 1808, and includes one of three Arab stallions: Darley Arabian, Byerley Turk or Godolphin Arabian. It is frequently crossed with other breeds and has been involved in the 'improvement' of some.

Unthrifty a horse which does not maintain good body condition despite receiving what would normally be adequate nutrition.

Withers slightly raised, bony area at the base of the neck between and above the shoulder bones.

Zebra stripes dark striping found on the insides of the legs of some horses and asses.

Index

Page numbers set in bold indicate illustration

ABORTION **47, 72, 76**
Acorns 58, 88-9
Age
  assessment 35-6
  problems 31, 35, 87, 90
Aggression
  behaviour 48-9, 52
  females 48, 49, 51, 55-6, 79
  foals 65, 77-82
  males 44, 45, 55, 83
  male and female 71, 74, 83
Agister 104-5, 106, 108, 109
Ailments
  anaemia 93
  blocked gut 86, 88, 98
  colic 86, 98, 119
  equine infectious anaemia 92
  influenza 90-91, 100
  laminitis 116
  pneumonia 90, 91
  poisoning 87-9
  strangles 90, 100
  tetanus 91, 108, 116
Arab 18, 23-4, 25, 29, 36, 125
Ass 7-8, 42, 56
Assateague Island 16-17, 44, 59, 60, 79, 82, 87, 92
Asturcon pony 19

BIRTH 75, 77, 98, 104
Bracken 58, 70, 87-8, 101
Breeding season 42, 46, 50, 51, 68, 75
British hill pony 21
Brumby 17, 44, 75

CAMARGUE 19, 50, 81, 97, 117
Celtic pony 21, 36
Coat
  composition 31-2
  condition 51, 66, 84, 93
  insulation **31**
  snow chute **32**
  water shedding 32, **33**
  whorls 32, **33**
Colostrum 76, 78

Common rights 21, 89, 104
Competition with man 8, 9, 14, 16, 17, 18, 123
Conception 47, 71, 75, 76, 79
Condition cycle 83-4
Connemara 28-9
Copulation 47, 73, **74**
Courtship 40, 72-3
Criollo horse 18

DALES PONY 26, 123
Dartmoor 22, **46**, 85, 87, 91, 95, 96, 104, 106, 108, 109-10, 111, 113, 120, 121, 123
Death 45, 84, 85, 88, 91, 92, 95, 98, 119, 120-22
Digestion 36, 61, 67, 86
Domestication 102
Dominance 44, 48, 49, 50-51, 55, 79
Donkey 8, 23, 42, 61
Drinking 60-61, 113
Dülmen pony 19
Dung (see also Latrines)
  analysis 67, 70
  composition 67, 70
  eating 60, 69
  frequency 67
  marking 40, **55**, 56, 68

EARS 37, 49, 52-4, 56, 62
Economics 114, 123
Eohippus 6
Eriskay pony 28, 123
Evolution 6, 10, 21
Exmoor 18, 21, 25-6, 32, 45, 46, 85, 91, 102, 107, 108, 109-10, 111, 113, 117, 120, 123
Extinction 7, 8, 9, 10, 11, 13

FAT RESERVES 57, 81, 83-4, 88
Feeding behaviour 57, 58, 59, 64, 81, 100
Fell pony 26
Feral horse 13, 15-19, 42, 123

Fertility 72, 79
Fighting 35, 43, 54, 56, **65**
Flehman **40**, 68, 73, 74,
Flies 81, **94**, 95-6, 97
  comfort behaviour 31, 51, 57, 63, 64, 92, 95, 96-7
  disease vectors 92, 95
  protection 31, 97
Foal
  bonding with dam 77, 78, 85
  fostering 78, 79
  killing 47
  management 17, 22, 45, 81
  rejection 78
  sex differences 65, 76, 81
  size 77
  stealing 79
  suckling 75, 78, 80-82
  survival 47, 71, 82, 85
Foal heat 79
Foods 37, 58-60, 70, 87, 88, 118
Fossilized ponies 7, 12, 21

GOWER PENINSULA 25, 45, 59, 92
Grooming **51**, 64, 65, 66, 96, 101
Groups
  bachelor **43**, 44, 45
  harem (band) **42**, 44, 45, 46, 48
  mares 45
  multi-stallion 43-4
  size 42, 43, 44
  temporary 46
  young 44

HERDING 51, **56**, 75
Highland pony **26**, 27
Home range 42, 43, 55, 85, 100
Hoof **41**, 110, 116

ICE AGE MOVEMENTS 7, 21
Immunity 90, 91, 100-101

Inbreeding 44, 45
Injury 45, 55, 56, 85, 114, 120

Jaws 35, 36, 38

Kaimanawa horse 17-18
Konig ponies 117

Lactation 60, 76, 81, 82, 84, 98
Latrines 69, 98
Legislation 18, 110, 113, 115
Lifespan 85
Locomotion 41
Lundy pony 28, 29
Lying down 62-3, 77

Malnutrition 76, 84
Management
  foals 22, 45, 81
  population control 16, 17, 18
  removal of poor stock 85, 110
  selective breeding 21, 22, 23, 25, 29, 36, 75, 123
  stallions 22, 23, 25, 45, 46
  supplementary feed 14, 85, 110
Marking
  brands 107-8, 109, 110, 111
  ear marks 108
  tail cutting 110, 111
Meat-eaters 61
Meat trade 9, 16, 18, 115
Medication 90, 91, 92, 93, 99, 100, 101, 116
Merens pony 19
Misaki horse 18
Mongolia 11, 12, 61
Mountain pony 21
Movements 51, 61, 64, 95
Mustang 15-16, 43, 44, 61, 75, 79
Mythology/folklore 61, 103

Native pony 13, 18, 19-28, 36
Natural selection 13, 45, 85, 101
New Forest 23, 29, 45, 46, 47, 48, 55, 58, 59, 68, 79, 85, 87, 89, 91, 95, 99, 104-6, 108, 109-11, 117, 120-22, 123

Oestrous 71-5, 79
Oestrous posture 72, 73, 74
Overgrazing 17, 18

Parasite, external (also see flies) 51, 66, 94
  lice 93
  midges 95
  ticks 93, 101
Parasite, internal 61, 67, 70, 86
  botfly larva 94, 96
  control 69, 99, 101, 110, 116
  pinworm 97, 99
  roundworm 97, 98
  tapeworm 97, 99
Perissodactyla 6
Pit ponies 22, 25
Play 43, 65-6, 81
Predators 30, 37, 77
Pregnancy 75, 76, 82, 98
Przewalski's horse 10-12
Puberty 71

Quagga 9-10

Rare breeds 26, 28, 123
Registration 22, 23, 24, 25, 107, 116
Reproduction rate 46-7, 71, 77
Rhum 27
Road accidents 25, 45, 104, 119, 120-22, 123
Rolling 66, 86, 95, 106
Roraima horse 18, 60
Rounding up 17, 19, 20, 91, 99, 109-10
Rubbing 66, 93, 95, 99

Sable Island 16, 42, 46, 57, 71, 75, 82, 85
Sales 22, 45, 110, 111, 113, 115-16
Salt 60
Senses
  hearing 37
  smell 39-40, 52, 68, 72, 73, 74, 79
  vision 37-8, 39
Sex ratio 43, 45, 46
Shackleford Island 17, 43

Shelter 16, 25, 42, 57, 59, 64
Shetland pony 22, 24, 27-8
Skyros pony 19
Sleep 54, 62, 63
Snapping (champing) 50
Social facilitation 51
Spanish influence 15, 18, 29
Stay mechanism 62
Steppe horse 21, 26, 27
Stress 82, 85, 92, 98, 108, 109, 111, 113, 116
Sweet itch 95
Sura pony 18

Tarpan 12-13, 19
Teeth 48
  dentition 6, 34-6, 81
  problems 35, 36, 84, 107
Temperature control 32-3, 63
Territoriality 42, 43, 56
Thoroughbred 23, 25, 75, 126

Urine 40, 56, 68, 69, 71, 72, 73, 74

Vigilance 37, 51
Vocalization 9, 54, 73

Weaning 17, 22, 80, 81-2, 116
Welfare organizations 106, 110, 113, 115
Welsh Mountain pony 18, 23-5, 29, 45, 108, 110, 111, 123

Zebra 9, 42, 56, 101